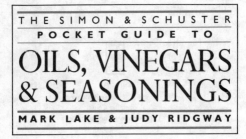

THE SIMON & SCHUSTER
POCKET GUIDE TO
OILS, VINEGARS & SEASONINGS

MARK LAKE & JUDY RIDGWAY

A Fireside Book
Published by Simon & Schuster Inc,
New York London Toronto Sydney Tokyo Singapore

FIRESIDE
Simon & Schuster Building
Rockefeller Center
1230 Avenue of the Americas
New York, New York 10020

The Simon & Schuster Pocket Guide to Oils, Vinegars & Seasonings
Edited and designed by Mitchell Beazley International Limited, Artists House,
14-15 Manette Street, London W1V 5LB.

FIRESIDE and colophon are registered trademarks
of Simon & Schuster Inc.

First published in Great Britain in 1989
by Mitchell Beazley Publishers under the title
The Mitchell Beazley Pocket Guide to Oils, Vinegars & Seasonings

1 3 5 7 9 10 8 6 4 2

Library of Congress Cataloging in Publication Data
available upon request

ISBN: 0-671-72896-2

Acknowledgments
The authors would like to thank the many people and organizations who have
helped with the research for this book. They are particularly grateful to the
International Olive Oil Council, Food and Wine from France and the Italian
Trade Centre. The books and articles of H. Magee, N. Arenillas and P. Antolini
provided other useful sorces of information.

Editor Rupert Joy
Designers Rupert Chappell, Joan Curtis
Production Stewart Bowling
Managing Editor Chris Foulkes
Senior Art Editor Tim Foster

Typeset by Litho Link, Welshpool, Powys, Wales
Produced by Mandarin Offset
Printed and bound in Malaysia

CONTENTS

GENERAL INTRODUCTION

GENERAL INTRODUCTION

Most people use oils, vinegars and seasonings every day. They are an essential part of our diet and, like many essentials, they are often taken for granted. Our purpose with this book is to show that oils, vinegars and seasonings are worth at least a second thought by everyone who takes an interest in what they eat. Even when used as staples their quality can determine the taste and flavour of a meal. When the best are chosen and cleverly used, they can transform good food into a gastronomic delight.

Today many people are bored with familiar taste experiences and ready to experiment with unusual products. However, as our interest in food flourishes, so too do the demands on our time, leaving less and less time available for food preparation. This does not mean that quality needs to be sacrificed. A careful use of high-quality flavourings can add interest and subtlety to even the simplest fare. Plain grilled meat, for example, can be completely transformed by pouring olive oil and a little lemon juice over it; in the same way, grilled fish improves immeasurably with the simple addition of a little almond oil.

The wine trade has gone to great lengths to educate us about wine: where it comes from, how it is made and how it tastes. There is just as much to learn about oils, vinegars and seasonings. Indeed, there are many connections between the two. Oils, vinegars and pastes are all manufactured either in or very near to the main wine-growing regions of the world. Olive trees and vines, moreover, require similar growing conditions and share similar methods of cultivation and production. Many wine-growers all over Europe also produce vinegar and olive oil, and have done for centuries.

Most of the ingredients in this book originate from Europe, particularly from the shores of the Mediterranean; this is, in fact, where the majority of Western culinary

4

traditions come from. These traditions and foods have gradually spread around the world and nowadays it is easy to forget their origins. But oils, vinegars and seasonings depend for their quality upon their origins. However hard manufacturers try to copy original products, mass-produced imitations never taste quite the same.

Growers and manufacturers have learned, often from centuries of experience, that the best possible product is never achieved by concentrating only on the basic ingredient. Methods of handling and blending are both vital to quality. This is why high-quality food and wine often come from the smaller producers: an individual can exert more control over small quantities. One of the main problems for the expanding producer is keeping the quality high as the volume increases; this is seldom easy to achieve. The best walnuts for oil-making, for example, come from the Dordogne – but they are expensive and there is not enough production to satisfy demand. As a result, other nuts have to be used from different areas in France.

The taste is, of course, the consumer's ultimate concern. The only way to learn about differences in taste is to experiment, by comparing and contrasting similar products. You might start by comparing olive oil with sunflower, soya or corn oil, and follow this by tasting olive oils from France, Spain, Greece and Italy. You could even go on to try varieties of olive oil from Liguria, Toscana (Tuscany) and Puglia (Apulia) which, although they are all Italian, are all subtly different. The sad fact about many of these unique European olive oils is that so few people are familiar with them. They do not know what they taste like or how to use them and opt, instead, for "safe" alternatives.

The production figures and nutritional information quoted for oils in this book are intended only as a rough guide. It is difficult to generalize because the nutritional content of an oil will vary depending on where it is produced. Equally, production figures for vegetable oils – especially for olive oil – vary considerably in each producing country from year to year. One further point to remember is that technological advances in the food industry are affecting both the production and the nutritional content of oils. Over the past few years, for example, the high level of erucic acid in rapeseed oil – which is considered harmful to health – has been reduced to a minimum.

The aim of this book is to help you discover and appreciate the difference between, for example, English and French mustard, roasted and unroasted sesame oil or wine and malt vinegar. The subject is a huge one and we have had to confine ourselves to the products most commonly used in Western kitchens – with, perhaps, a little extra emphasis on our own favourites. Unfortunately, there simply is not room to include every type of oil or every type of herb, but we hope our suggestions will encourage you to experiment and even to make further discoveries of your own.

Choosing oils, vinegars and seasonings

We strongly believe that chemical flavourings are unnecessary in cooking. Sea salt or rock salt are preferable to a chemical free-flowing salt, just as wine vinegar is preferable to a non-brewed condiment. Monosodium glutamate is another flavour-enhancer which is best avoided. It was originally derived from seaweed, but is now produced commercially from sugarbeet pulp and wheat.

The consumer is usually forced to rely on the labelling and packaging of the product in making a choice of oils, vinegars and seasonings. Labels can help you to find quality products which are stable without chemical additives – but beware the word "pure". This is not an indication of quality or taste. It simply means that nothing has been added and it may mean that it has passed through heavy processing. Packaging also creates an important impression, but it does not guarantee the quality of the product. The only way to be certain of the quality is to rely on the reputation of the producer, or to taste the product for yourself.

OILS

INTRODUCTION

There are five basic types of nutrients in foods. These are proteins, carbohydrates, vitamins, minerals and fats. Oils are fats. The only difference between oils and fats as they usually appear is that fats are solid at room temperature and oils are liquid.

As well as providing essential nutrients for body-building and energy, oils are important because they carry much of the flavour of food. In cooking they improve the texture of food and assist in lubrication; they are also efficient at transferring heat. In addition, oils have important industrial uses in applications as diverse as cosmetics, paints, plastics, soaps and insecticides.

Vegetable oils may be extracted from the crushed whole fruit of the plant, as in the case of olive oil, from nuts as in the case of nut oils and coconut oil, or from beans and seeds, as in the case of soya, sunflower and rapeseed oil.

OIL PRODUCTION

Olive oil was probably the first oil to be produced on a commercial scale. Olive trees have always grown well in the Mediterranean climate; from there they spread and now flourish in similar climates elsewhere. In countries where the climate is less conducive to oil-producing crops, animal fats have traditionally provided the main source of fat. However, with the growth of interest in alternatives to animal fats for reasons of health, convenience and economy, new industries have sprung up to produce oils from all kinds of other sources.

CHEMISTRY OF OILS

Oils are made up of triglycerides. Each triglyceride consists of one molecule of glycerol to which three fatty acid molecules are attached. Any unattached fatty acid molecules in the oil are called free fatty acids. It is the percentage of these free fatty acids present in an oil which will determine the oil's acidity level.

There are around 20 fatty acids which occur naturally in oils; they give oils and fats their unique properties. Fatty acids are made up of carbon atoms arranged in long chains. If the fatty acid has no double bonds and is full up with hydrogen, it is called a saturated fatty acid.

Saturated fatty acid

```
H           H           H           H           H
|           |           |           |           |
C     —     C     —     C     —     C     —     C
|           |           |           |           |
H           H           H           H           H
```

If on the other hand a fatty acid has one or more double bonds and room for more hydrogen atoms in its chain, it is called an unsaturated fatty acid. Where there is only one double bond in the chain, it is a monounsaturated fatty acid; where there is more than one double bond, it is a polyunsaturated fatty acid.

Unsaturated fatty acid

```
H                                   H           H
|                                   |           |
C     —     C     =     C     —     C     —     C
|                                   |           |
H         double bond               H           H
```

The double bonds in unsaturated fatty acid molecules make room for other substances to be added to the chain. If oxygen is added, the fat becomes rancid; if hydrogen is added, the fat becomes saturated. These bonds can also be used by the human body to add other nutrients, which help it to build cells.

Animal fats tend to be rich in saturated fatty acids, but vegetable oils vary considerably in their make-up. Some vegetable oils have a high percentage of polyunsaturated fatty acids; others, like olive oil, are rich in monounsaturates. A few have a high percentage of saturated fatty acids. For more details, see the chart on page 11.

The more unsaturated a fat is, the more it is prone to deterioration. This is because the make-up of its molecular chain is such that it absorbs oxygen more readily than saturated fat.

Temperature changes

Many oils crystallize at a temperature of less than 5°C and form a solid mass. As they are heated, the crystals melt and the solid liquifies. As the oil melts, it thins and expands.

When oils are heated beyond a certain temperature, they will start to break down. However, oils can take a considerable amount of heat before this deterioration occurs. Many oils are quite stable at 200°C. The characteristic sign of breakdown is a blue haze rising off the fat – the "smoke point". If an oil is allowed to overheat for too long, its temperature will rise to the point when it catches fire.

SMOKE POINTS FOR HOUSEHOLD OILS		
Main types of household oils	°C	°F
Corn oil	210	410
Grapeseed oil	230	446
Ground-nut oil	210	410
Olive oil	210	410
Rapeseed oil	225	437
Soya oil	210	410
Sunflower oil	200	392

The oils in the table above are all suitable for deep-frying. Some of the specialized oils like the nut oils and oriental sesame oil do not have such high smoke points and should be used for flavouring rather than frying.

Emulsions

An emulsion is a liquid which comprises one liquid, dispersed in small droplets in another liquid. If you mix oil and water together, the oil will float to the top of the water. If they are beaten together with a whisk, they will form a cloudy, possibly thickish liquid. After a few minutes, however, the two will begin to separate again. Vinaigrette is an example of just such an unstable emulsion.

To form a stable emulsion, some type of emulsifying agent like mustard or egg yolk must be added. In commercial vinaigrettes, the only difference between those which separate in the bottle and those which do not is that one has had a commercial emulsifier added to it. Mayonnaise, which is made with oil, vinegar and egg yolks, is naturally fairly stable. Here the emulsifying agent is the lecithin found in the egg yolks.

Rancidity

Rancidity is caused by oxidation. The oxygen in the air gets into the oil container and is taken up by the fatty acid molecules. This process is accelerated in unsaturated oils. Light and salt also accelerate the absorption of oxygen. Oxidation breaks up the oil, producing unpleasant smells and tastes. Vitamin E, a natural antioxident present in some fresh oils like sunflower, safflower and olive oil, delays the onset of oxidation.

The degree to which an oil is likely to be affected by rancidity can be measured by using iodine, which determines the number of double bonds in the fatty acids. The higher the iodine value, the higher the number of double bonds and the more likely the oil is to go rancid.

OILS AND NUTRITION

The body can manufacture for itself most of the fatty acids which we eat in our food. However, there are three which the body cannot make – linoleic acid, arachidonic acid and linolenic acid. These, the "essential" fatty acids, are all unsaturated and found exclusively in vegetable oils.

Most oils are also good sources of vitamin E, but they do vary in their vitamin E content and there is also a variable loss during refining. Safflower and sunflower oil can contain very high levels. These are followed by cottonseed, palm, corn and rapeseed oils. Some contain traces of protovitamin A (carotene) and minerals such as iodine. Vegetable oils do not contain any fibre or cholesterol.

There is little loss of nutritive value when oils are used in baking, but polyunsaturated oils do decline when they are heated for frying. There is no evidence that rancid oils or oils which have been overheated in the home are a danger to health. However, such oils will not contain any vitamin E or any polyunsaturated fatty acids.

Energy

Oils and fats are the richest source of energy in a diet. Slimmers should note that they can be far more fattening than carbohydrates or starchy foods such as bread, pasta and rice. Weight for weight, fats can produce at least twice as much energy. All oils produce exactly the same amount of energy – 370 kilojoules or 90 kilocalories per tablespoon (10ml/⅓fl oz). So-called "light" oils do not mean less energy, but simply less flavour.

OILS AND HEART DISEASE

Today the use of vegetable oils in cookery is well-established throughout the Western world. However, apart from the Mediterranean countries which have always produced and consumed a large quantity of olive oil, this is a relatively modern phenomenon.

One reason for the upsurge in the use of vegetable oils in the West is growing health-consciousness. Medical and dietary authorities have labelled fat, particularly saturated fat, as one element responsible for coronary heart disease, which is becoming more frequent in developed countries.

FATTY ACID TYPES IN DIFFERENT OILS			
*Average percentages**			
Types of oil	Polyun-saturated fat	Monoun-saturated fat	Saturated fat
Almond oil	16.0	76.0	7.5
Avocado oil	3.0	80.0	10.0
Coconut oil	2.5	7.5	90.0
Corn oil	43.5	43.0	11.0
Cottonseed oil	48.5	25.0	25.5
Grapeseed oil	73.5	0.1	7.5
Ground-nut oil	29.5	53.5	7.0
Hazelnut oil	18.5	76.0	7.5
Mustard oil	21.5	74.0	0.2
Olive oil	12.0	69.5	16.0
Palm oil	8.5	44.0	50.0
Palm kernel oil	18.0	13.5	59.5
Pistachio oil	20.0	69.0	8.0
Pumpkinseed oil	40.0	35.0	12.0
Rapeseed oil	20.0	55.0	6.0
Safflower oil	70.5	22.5	7.5
Sesame oil	38.0	45.5	8.0
Soya oil	43.5	37.0	14.0
Sunflower oil	59.5	28.5	11.0
Walnut oil	71.0	16.5	9.5

*Because different versions of the same oil vary so much in their fatty acid content, these figures are based on the median of the figures quoted elsewhere in the book.

The COMA Panel Report on diet and cardiovascular disease published in the UK in July 1984 echoed world medical opinion by recommending a cut in the total amount of fat consumed and a move towards the consumption of more unsaturated fat in place of saturated fat. One reason for these recommendations was that blood cholesterol levels, which show a strong correlation to heart disease, seem to be directly related to dietary fat consumption. It has been shown that diets rich in saturated fats and cholesterol contribute to high cholesterol in the blood. Consumption of polyunsaturated fats, on the other hand, leads to a significant reduction in blood cholesterol.

However, more recent research has shown that there are two types of cholesterol in the blood: HDL (high-density lipoprotein) cholesterol and LDL (low-density lipoprotein) cholesterol. HDL cholesterol is regarded as beneficial to the body in that it helps eliminate artery-clogging fats, while LDL cholesterol is thought to encourage fatty deposits.

Polyunsaturated fats lower the general cholesterol level in the body, but this means that the beneficial HDL cholesterol is reduced as well as the LDL cholesterol. Monounsaturated fats seem to be more discerning in that they lower LDL cholesterol levels while promoting higher levels of HDL cholesterol. So some cardiac surgeons recommend a fat intake of one-third saturated fat, one-third monounsaturated fat and one-third polyunsaturated fat.

These conclusions also reflect the results of research into the incidence of cardiovascular disease in different countries. Studies have shown that cardiovascular problems occur least in the Mediterranean countries and are at their highest in countries such as the USA, Finland and Scotland. It was found that the only dietary variation between the two geographical groups consisted in the kind of fat eaten. In the United States, people consume mainly saturated fats whereas in the Mediterranean countries they tend to consume mainly monounsaturated fats or olive oil.

COOKING WITH OILS

In cooking, oils are used mainly for frying and for lubricating prior to roasting or grilling. They are widely used in dressings and cold sauces, and they can also be used in baking.

Oils also make excellent flavourings. Meat or fish can be fried in a bland oil like sunflower oil and then flavoured with an extra virgin olive oil, or with one of the nut oils. Brush pork or lamb chops with these oils before grilling. Add a small amount of the stronger oils like pineseed oil, roasted sesame oil or pistachio oil to stir-fry dishes.

Frying with oils

Vegetable oils are excellent for frying. They can be heated to a temperature of 200°C or more without deteriorating and they are highly efficient at transferring heat to food. Frying works by sealing the outside of the food very quickly. This prevents moisture from escaping and oil from soaking in: the food inside the seal is virtually cooked in its own steam.

Whether food is pan-fried or deep-fried, the oil must be at the correct temperature. If the temperature is too low, the food will be soggy and greasy; if it is too high, the food will darken on the outside before the centre is cooked and the oil will break down more rapidly.

Ideally, the oil should be heated up fairly slowly and a thermometer used to test for the correct temperature at which different foods should be cooked.

FRYING TEMPERATURES FOR DIFFERENT FOODS		
Assorted deep-fried foods	**°C**	**°F**
Large chicken joints, cutlets, vegetables	160	320
Battered or breaded fish, small chicken joints, fruit fritters	170	338
Onion rings, doughnuts	180	356
Potato chips	190	374

If you do not have an electric deep-fat fryer or a kitchen thermometer, oil temperature can be tested by frying a 2½cm cube of day-old bread for one minute, after which it should be crisp and an even golden colour.

Some dos and don'ts for deep-fat frying

■ Cut the food uniformly to prevent small pieces burning before the larger pieces are cooked.

■ Fill the deep-fat fryer only about one-third full with oil. If you overload it, oil will boil over the sides when food is added to the pan.

■ The recommended ratio of oil to food is about 3:1. If this is exceeded, the temperature of the oil will fall and the food will not cook properly. If you have a large quantity of food to fry, cook it in batches.

■ Unbattered and uncoated food should be drained and dried before being added to the oil. The addition of excess water into the fryer will cause splashing as well as a faster deterioration of the oil.

■ With the exception of chips and some coated fish, avoid taking food straight from the freezer to the deep-fat fryer.

■ Shake off any excess batter or coating from the food before adding to the oil. Bits and pieces which fall off the food may burn and cause deterioration of the oil.

■ Salt the food after frying, not before.

■ Strain off the oil after frying and store for further use. A good quality oil can be used up to a dozen times if the above points are observed.

If an unregulated fat fryer is left on the heat, the temperature of the oil will go on rising until it catches fire. If this happens, the fire can be extinguished by smothering the flames with the lid or with an asbestos cloth.

NEVER ATTEMPT TO MOVE THE PAN AND NEVER USE WATER TO TRY TO EXTINGUISH THE BURNING OIL. This will make matters worse by causing the burning oil to explode.

Storing oil

Store oil in an airtight container in a cool place away from the light. Although only a laboratory analysis can show conclusively whether an oil has gone off or broken down, there are a number of signs to look for which show when an oil is coming to the end of its useful life:

■ The oil develops a rancid smell or smells of stale cooking.
■ The oil starts to foam excessively when food is added.
■ The oil darkens and smokes excessively on heating.

OLIVE OIL

Olive oil is produced from the fruit of the olive tree *Olea Europea*. The exact origins of this tree are not known, though its history is tied up with that of the Mediterranean. However, it is generally agreed that the olive originated in Asia Minor and Crete; it was certainly being cultivated in the eastern Mediterranean as long ago as 3,000 BC.

The Greeks spread the cultivation of the olive tree throughout the Mediterranean; they introduced it into the South of France and probably before that into Italy. The fact that the tree grew well on poor soil and produced a durable fruit which was highly nutritious helped the inhabitants of many countries to survive famines.

The olive tree was growing in Africa when the Romans arrived. They spread olive cultivation and the use of olive oil throughout their large empire, including the Iberian peninsula. Later Romans imported considerable quantities of olive oil from Spain, as the Italians do today. During the 16th century, the Spanish continued the expansion of olive oil production by bringing olive trees to the Americas. By the end of the century, the olive was well established in Peru, Chile, Argentina, Mexico, California and the West Indies. Today the olive tree may be found wherever the climate is suitable for its growth.

Physical properties of olive oil	
Solidification point	2°C
Melting point	5-7°C
Smoke point	210°C
Weight	1 litre = 910-916 grams
Nutritional values of olive oil*	
Saturated fatty acids: mainly palmitic acid	8-23.5%
Monounsaturated fatty acids: mainly oleic acid	56-83%
Polyunsaturated fatty acids: mainly linoleic acid	3.5-20%
linolenic acid	trace
Iodine value	75-94
Vitamin content	vitamin E/protovitamin A

*The wide range in the percentage levels of different fatty acid types is due to the large number of different olive varieties.

14

OLIVE CULTIVATION

Most of the world's olive oil is produced around the shores of the Mediterranean. Olive trees flourish in the Mediterranean climate with its mild winter, wet spring and autumn, and dry hot summer. They do not like damp or cold and temperatures below 10 °C can easily kill them. Indeed, the unusually bitter winters of 1956 and 1984 destroyed many of the Spanish and Tuscan olive groves.

The olive tree does not need rich fertile soil and is planted mainly on poor stony ground which is unsuitable for most other crops. Greece and Italy are ideal for growing olives. They both have regions of high rocky mountains which are are almost inaccessible, but which can sustain a crop that does not need much looking after. The olive can grow at an altitude of up to 400 metres.

Olives

The olive tree

The main sub-species of *Olea Europea* is *Euromediterranea*. The two principal trees within this sub-species are *Sativa* and *Oleaster*. *Sativa* is the cultivated olive tree which can now be found all over the world. *Oleaster* is a wild, prickly tree with small fruit which grows in the Mediterranean region.

The olive is an evergreen tree with a short twisted trunk dividing into thick, uneven branches. It is characterized by its gnarled apprearance and it is not unusual for a tree to live a hundred years. The leaves are dark green on the top side and covered with silvery scales on the underside. The fruit is drop- or pear-shaped. It is green when unripe, changing to a dark brown or black colour when the fruit ripens. The harvest for green olives is September to November and for black olives from November to February.

The olive takes four or five years to grow into a tree and it yields its first fruit at this age, but it will not reach its full fruit-bearing capacity until it is 20 years old or more. From then on the yield remains much the same until it dies. This slow build-up to maturation means that it is impossible to make up for a shortfall in one year's production rapidly by planting extra groves as, for example, seed oil producers can do with crops of rape or sunflower.

Harvesting

This takes place in late autumn and winter. Olive-picking is an expensive business as no one has yet found a perfect method of getting the olives off the tree. There are machines which shake the tree, but this is not always ideal. The olives naturally drop to the ground when ripe and they can then be gathered up, but the most popular method is to spread nets either directly onto the ground or onto small stakes, which keep the olives away from the heat of the ground. Men on ladders with poles and rakes knock the olives off the branches into the nets.

OLIVE OIL PRODUCTION

After harvesting, the olives are taken to the oil mill where they are stored for anything between a few hours and a few days. This storage process allows the olives to heat up a little naturally, but not enough for them to ferment. The slight heat helps to release the oil from the pulp.

The olives are washed in cold water and crushed. This breaks the cells of the fruit, releasing the oil. Large stone wheels are used to churn the olives to pulp. The milling time varies depending on the type of olive, but the result is a smooth paste without any lumps. Usually the stones are broken in the pulp, but some mills de-stone before milling.

The olive paste is spread on esparto fibre mats or discs in layers weighing about five kilos each. These are stacked together and placed in the press, following a method which has been used for centuries. The expression "cold pressed" olive oil comes from this process. The pressure is not too high and this stops heat from building up in the paste. (Heat would bring out more oil but would also change its taste.)

The liquid that comes out of the press is a dark reddish green. It is a mixture of oil, vegetable matter and water. In the old days, the oil was racked off from the water, but nowadays the liquid is put into a centrifuge. The older method can still be seen in parts of Italy where racking is done by hand. The oil is put into large amphorae standing one and a half metres high. At this stage, there is still a great deal of sediment suspended in the oil. When the temperature of the oil rises in the spring, the oil thins and all the sediment is deposited in the bottom of the amphorae.

The average yield is 2.5-3 litres of olive oil per tree. Five kilos of olives give approximately one litre of oil. Most of the oil produced by cold pressing, up to 90 per cent, will be virgin olive oil; the remaining oil is Lampante virgin olive oil. The oil that is extracted from the cake of dry paste is called olive residue oil.

Lampante virgin olive oil is refined to reduce its colour, smell and flavour, and to lower the acidity. The oil is known as refined olive oil, but more usually it is blended with virgin olive oil to be called pure olive oil.

Hot water is mixed with the remaining oil cake. The mixture is put through a centrifuge and pressed for a second time. This is second pressing oil. None of the small growers do this; they tend to send their cake away to the co-operatives. Here the oil cake is subjected to solvents which extract the remaining oil, about one per cent. This oil, having been refined, can be sold only as refined olive-residue oil. Most of it goes for industrial use.

Many countries are researching less labour-intensive methods of oil extraction and there has been interest in using a new type of centrifuge instead of a press. More automation is needed, but given the problems involved it will be some time before this is widely introduced.

WORLD PRODUCTION AND CONSUMPTION

About 800 million olive trees grow around the Mediterranean – that is 93 per cent of the world's olive trees. These produce just under eight million tonnes of olives, of which over 90 per cent are used for oil production and the rest sold as table olives.

World production in a very good year may be just under two million tonnes, but in a poor year less than half this. The average annual world production is about one and a half million tonnes.

Well over half of the world's olive oil in a typical year is produced by Spain and Italy. Roughly one-third of world production comes from Greece, Tunisia, Turkey, Portugal, Morocco and Syria. The rest comes from other countries in the Mediterranean region, the Middle East and the Americas.

The world production figures for olive oil represent only five per cent of the total production of vegetable oil. Soya oil accounts for 42 per cent, followed by rapeseed oil and sunflower oil. Olive oil is more expensive because of the high cost of harvesting and production.

About 92 per cent of the olive oil produced is consumed in the producer countries. Greece consumes 23 litres per head per year, while Italy and Spain manage about 10 litres each. The French, however, consume only 0.4 litres per

OLIVE OIL PRODUCING COUNTRIES OF THE WORLD

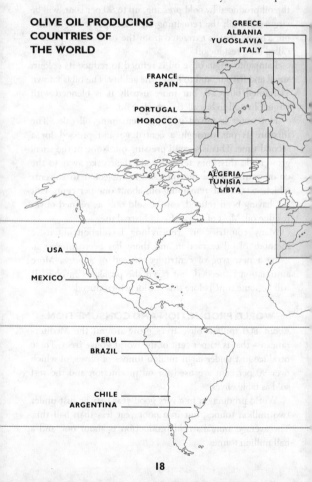

head annually, and consumption in both the UK and the USA is only 0.2 litres per head per year.

WORLD PRODUCTION FIGURES FOR OLIVE OIL BY COUNTRY OF ORIGIN, 1987/88 (Figures are in thousand tonnes.)			
Spain	697	Portugal	39
Italy	583	Morocco	39
Greece	225	Syria	31
Tunisia	117	France	2
Turkey	69	Others	65
WORLD TOTAL			**1,867**

Production and consumption in the EEC

Since the accession of Greece to the EEC in 1981, the community has become self-sufficient in terms of olive oil.

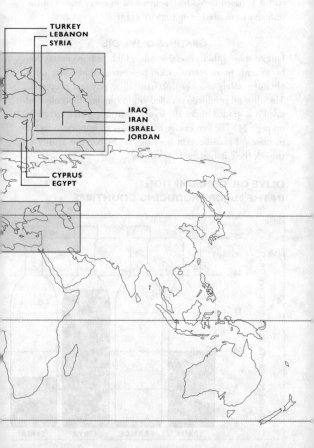

The olive is a perennial crop and trees can last for a hundred years. Olive cultivation is a valuable heritage and it is essential for the natural environment and the social stability of many regions. There are about 500 million olive trees in the EEC, covering six million hectares, and about one million families depend either entirely or partly on olive-growing for their subsistence.

Most olive oils on sale in the UK come from Spain, Italy and Greece, the three largest producers in the world, and from France, although it is a much smaller producer.

The International Olive Oil Council

This is an organization set up to help solve any problems arising in the world olive oil economy and to promote research and development in the industry. The council, which is based in Madrid, is involved in every aspect of the industry from marketing to price control.

GRADING OLIVE OIL

Unlike most other vegetable oils which require extraction by solvents or re-esterification processes, edible olive oil is obtained solely through mechanical or physical processes. The olive oil produced is called virgin (unclassified) olive oil until it is graded under the legal definitions which are given on page 21. The percentage of acidity is an important factor in olive oil classification because the higher the acidity of the oil, the harsher the taste will be.

OLIVE OIL CONSUMPTION IN THE MAJOR PRODUCING COUNTRIES

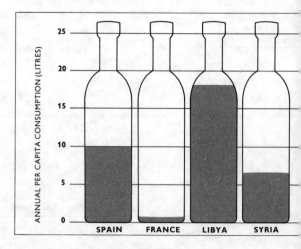

Extra virgin olive oil

For olive oil to be graded as extra virgin olive oil, it must meet the following requirements:

■ Perfect flavour
■ Perfect aroma
■ Perfect colour (light yellow to green)
■ Maximum acidity of one per cent

Fine virgin olive oil

For olive oil to be graded as fine virgin olive oil, it must meet the following requirements:

■ Perfect colour
■ Perfect aroma
■ Perfect colour (light yellow to green)
■ Maximum acidity of 1.5 per cent

Semi-fine virgin olive oil

For olive oil to be graded as semi-fine virgin olive oil, or simply labelled as virgin olive oil, it must meet these requirements:

■ Acceptable flavour
■ Acceptable aroma
■ Acceptable colour (light yellow to green)
■ Maximum acidity of three per cent

Lampante virgin olive oil

This is off-flavour oil, or olive oil with an acidity of more than 3.3 per cent.

Pure olive oil

For olive oil to be graded as pure olive oil, it must meet the following requirements:

■ Good flavour
■ Good aroma

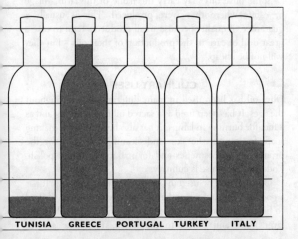

TUNISIA   GREECE   PORTUGAL   TURKEY   ITALY

■ Good colour (light yellow)
■ Maximum acidity of 1.5 per cent

Pure olive oil is derived from a blending of extra virgin olive oil and refined olive oil.

Refined olive oil

Refined olive oil is produced from virgin olive oil by methods which do not alter the chemical structure of the oil. These methods include washing, decantation, centrifugation and filtration.

Residue olive oil

This is crude oil obtained by treating the olive pulp with solvents and refining the oil. Residue olive oils are used in the soap industry.

Labels

In practice, the only descriptions likely to be found on labels in the shops are extra virgin olive oil and pure olive oil. Occasionally, however, you may come across bottles marked simply virgin olive oil.

All olive oil labels must show the grade of olive oil in the bottle, together with its acidity level, volume, country of origin and producer's name. The label may also carry the words "first pressing" or "first cold pressing". This wording, which will be found only on bottles of extra virgin olive oil, means literally what it says: the bottle contains only oil from the first pressing. Alternatively, the label may carry the words "cold pressing". This means that the pressure used to extract the oil has been kept to a minimum; if heavy presses are used, the temperature will rise, impairing the quality of the oil.

Some olive oils may carry the name of the farm, village or estate where they were produced. This is usually a guarantee of quality because small producers tend to take a great deal of care in the production of their oils – but they will not be cheap.

CULINARY USES

Olive oil has been used in many different ways throughout the ages. It has been used as a sacred oil for anointing and as a fuel for burning in lamps; it has also been used for making soap, for toning the skin and cleaning the hair, for the production of cosmetics and for making furniture polish. Today, its main use is culinary.

Olive oil may be used in place of butter in cooking. It has a good flavour and a wonderful aroma when heated. It used to be claimed in France that olive oil was used south of the river Loire and butter to the north. The same sort of culinary divide also occurs in northern and southern Italy, except that in the northern butter-producing region, olive oil is used alongside butter in cooking.

Uncooked, olive oil is principally used in salads to give a fruity taste to dressings. It is also used in many Mediterranean countries as a sauce. After the meat is grilled over an open fire, a little lemon juice is squeezed onto the hot meat; this is followed by a trickle of virgin olive oil. It is also used to finish off soups, dips and stews. The heat of the food brings out the flavour of the oil and this blends in with the full flavours of the dish.

The taste of olive oil

Olive oil has a great variety of flavours. There are hundreds of different types of olive tree, with hundreds of different names: many areas use local names for trees that may have other names when grown in another country or continent. There are even different spellings for names within the same country. This is further complicated by the fact that many trees are grafted onto different root stocks and grown in different climates or by different methods of cultivation.

As with wine-tasting, it is very difficult to describe the different tastes of olive oil. However, it is possible to make the following generalizations:

■ Its colour ranges from pale yellow to dark green.
■ Its taste is generally described as fruity light/heavy.
■ In terms of weight, olive oil is described as having a light or heavy feel in the mouth.
■ An olive smells either light/subtle or heavy/obvious.

French oil is considered light in taste with great subtlety. It lacks the taste of the sun noticeable in the oils of more southerly climates. Italy produces some of the best oils in the world, particularly from the single estates. The oils are medium to heavy in weight and tending to green in colour, with great complexities of taste. Spain produces oils which tend to be yellow and heavy; they usually also have a taste of the sun. Greece produces oils which have a pronounced green colour and a medium weight. Although they do not have any great complexity of taste, they are extremely good value for money. There are, of course, many exceptions in every country. The only real way to choose between olive oils is to start tasting for yourself.

ITALIAN OLIVE OIL

With the exception of the Po Valley, Italy is extremely mountainous. This is ideal terrain for olive groves. Olives are widely cultivated in all the coastal areas of the country, mainly in the central and southern regions, and in the islands of Sicilia (Sicily) and Sardegna (Sardinia). The main olive-producing regions are Puglia (Apulia) and Calabria in southern Italy.

In a typical year, Italian olive oil production might be distributed among the main producing regions as follows:

Puglia (Apulia)	40%	Abruzzi	3%
Calabria	30%	Basilicata	2%
Sicilia (Sicily)	11%	Toscana (Tuscany)	2%
Campania	5%	Other regions	7%

1. ABRUZZI
2. BASILICATA
3. CALABRIA
4. CAMPANIA
5. EMILIA-ROMAGNA
6. FRIULI-VENEZIA GIULIA
7. LAZIO
8. LIGURIA
9. LOMBARDIA
10. MARCHE
11. MOLISE
12. PUGLIA
13. SARDEGNA
14. SICILIA
15. TOSCANA
16. TRENTINO-ALTO ADIGE
17. UMBRIA
18. VENETO

24

In this last decade the weather has played a large part in Italy's production difficulties. In 1984, many of the olive trees, particularly in Toscana (Tuscany), were killed by frost and it will be years before production is back to normal.

Italy used to be one of the main exporters of olive oil, but now it imports more than it exports. Although Italy still produces a large quantity of olive oil, it does not produce enough in the lower grades, so it imports foreign oils and blends them with its own. Thus, not all of the oil exported from Italy is of Italian origin, even though the label is Italian. This practice fully conforms with Italian laws, but it does rather complicate matters.

The oils of Italy have an extremely good, fruity flavour. However, the taste of the oils can change from one year to the next, depending on the weather. One of the other factors which changes the taste is the variety of olive tree. The principal Italian varieties are *Coratina, Cellina Dinardo, Sinopolese, Frantoio, Ogliarolo Barese, Ogliarolo Leccese, Leccino, Moraiolo, Cima di Mola* and *Nicastrese*.

Abruzzi
Production here is concentrated on Chieti, Pescara and Teramo. The region's olive varieties include *Leccino, Moraiolo, Cavazzana* and *Cerasolo*.

Basilicata
This area is another large producer of olive oil. The main varieties are *Coratina, Nostrale* and *Rotondella*.

Calabria
This is the second-largest producer of olive oil in Italy, although only a small amount of extra virgin oil is produced in the region. Production is concentrated around Reggio, Catanzaro and Cosenza. The main varieties grown are *Sinopolese, Goccitano* and *Cerasolo*.

Campania
This is another major producer. The main area of production is around Salerno. Varieties include *Rotondella, Leccino, Frantoio, Olivolo* and *Olivella*.

Lazio (Latium)
The area which produces the best olive oil in this region is centred on the hills around Rome. Varieties include *Rosciola, Frantoio* and many others.

Liguria
This is a small region producing light, fruity oils. The best oil comes from around Imperia. The main variety is *Taggiasca*.

Molise
This is a small producer. The main varieties include *Leccino* and *Coratino*.

Puglia (Apulia)

Apulia is the largest producer of olive oil in Italy. The greatest concentration of olive trees is around Bari. This region produces extremely good extra virgin oil, mainly from the *Coratina* olive variety.

Sardegna (Sardinia)

Oil produced here is mainly used locally. Olives are mostly grown along the coast. The main variety is *Bosana*.

Sicilia (Sicily)

This is a large producer of olive oil. Production is concentrated on the western half of the island around Palermo, Trapani and Agrigento. Varieties include *Bincolilla, Ogliarolo* and *Cerasolo*.

Toscana (Tuscany)

There are olive groves covering the whole region. Tuscany produces about 25,000 tonnes annually. Varieties include *Frantoio, Moraiolo* and *Leccino*.

Although Tuscany is a small producing region, its olive oil is widely known and appreciated outside Italy, partly due to a long marketing operation. There is also careful quality control and a consortium to look after both the producers and the consumers.

Lucca has the reputation for the best oil, but the oils from Chianti, Colli Senese, Pisa and Prato are just as good, if not better. Taken as a whole, Tuscany produces more extra virgin olive oil than any other region. Tuscan oils tend to be greener than their counterparts in the south.

Umbria

This is a small producing region, but like its neighbour, Tuscany, the quality is high. The best areas are Trasimento and Spoleto. The main variety is *Moraiolo*.

The rest of Italy

Good oil is produced in small quantities elsewhere in Marche (the Marches), Veneto (Venetia), Emilia-Romagna, Lombardia (Lombardy), Friuli-Venezia Giulia and finally Trentino-Alto Adige. The olive groves in Trentino are the most northerly in Europe.

SPANISH OLIVE OIL

Spain is one of the largest producers of olive oil. In some years, it tops the world production charts; in other years, Italy produces more.

The Spanish word for olive oil is *Aceite,* from an Arabic word meaning "olive juice". There are just under two hundred million olive trees in Spain, occupying some two million hectares.

In a typical year, Spanish olive oil production might be distributed among the main producing regions as follows:

Jaén	36%	Alicante	1%
Córdoba	13%	Badajoz	1%
Málaga	6%	Huelva	1%
Granada	5%	Madrid	1%
Sevilla (Seville)	3%	Zaragoza (Saragossa)	1%
Toledo	3%	Valencia	1%
Tarragona	3%	Huesca	1%
Ciudad Real	3%	Teruel	1%
Lérida	1%	Cáceres	1%
Castellón	1%	Other regions	17%

Spain has a large number of olive varieties and it is difficult to separate the different varieties from those which simply go by alternative local names in the various Spanish districts. However, the principal olive varieties are *Blanqueta, Gordal, Picudo, Hojiblanca, Verdeña, Farga, Manzanilla, Picolimón, Cornicabra, Navadillo, Lechín, Carrasqueña, Picual, Verdial de Badajoz* and *Cacereña*.

Quality olive oils

Certain regions in Spain produce exceptionally high-quality olive oils, and have their own labels of origin. The governing body for the Spanish olive oil industry, the *Instituto Nacional de Denominaciónes de Origen* (I.N.D.O.), recognizes four labels of origin in Cataluña (Catalonia) and Andalucia (Andalusia): Borjas Blancas, Siurana, Sierra de Segura and Baena. Other areas applying for recognition are Castro del Rio, Priego, Puente-Genil, Carcabuey and Alcañiz.

Alicante

The olive groves in this region cover 21,000 hectares. They produce oils with a low acidity, a mild aroma, a fruity taste and a colour which varies from pale yellow to golden. The main olive varieties in Alicante are *Blanqueta, Manzanilla, Cuquillo* and *Gordal*.

Badajoz

This is one of Spain's main olive-growing regions with 187,000 hectares producing both olive oil and table olives. It produces good oil with a sweet taste, a fruity aroma and a yellow colour. The main varieties are *Verdial de Badajoz, Morisca, Cornezuelo* and *Manzanilla*.

Cáceres

The olive groves in this region cover 79,000 hectares. They produce oils of a fairly high acidity, which are mild, fruity and golden. The main varieties are *Cacereña, Verdial, Corniche* and *Cordobi*.

OILS

(1) ALICANTE
(2) BADAJOZ
(3) CÁCERES
(4) CASTELLÓN
(5) CIUDAD REAL
(6) CÓRDOBA
(7) GRANADA

(8) HUELVA
(9) HUESCA
(10) JAÉN
(11) LÉRIDA
(12) MADRID
(13) MÁLAGA
(14) SEVILLA

(15) TARRAGONA
(16) TERUEL
(17) TOLEDO
(18) VALENCIA
(19) ZARAGOZA

Castellón

This region has a terrain of plain and mountain slopes, covered by 38,000 hectares of olive groves. It produces an oil which is full, fruity and yellow. The main varieties are *Farga* and *Morrut Roig.*

Ciudad Real

The oil produced in this region is fruity and golden yellow. The main variety is *Cornicabra.*

Córdoba

This region, with olive groves covering 295,000 hectares, has a terrain which varies from mountains to plains. The best-quality oils are from Baena and Puente-Genil.

Baena, which has its own label of origin, is the southern province of Córdoba, and has 32,000 hectares of olive groves. It has a sub-continental climate with dry, hot summers. Production is largely for the home market. The main olive varieties cultivated in Baena are *Picudo, Picual, Hojiblanca* and *Lechín.*

Castel del Rio and Priego are also in southern Córdoba. The oil produced here is pale yellow and fruity. A third of production in these areas goes for export.

Granada

The olive groves in this region cover 110,000 hectares. The main varieties are *Lechín, Picudo, Picual* and *Hojiblanca.*

Huelva

The olive groves in this region cover 30,000 hectares. The main varieties are *Verdial de Huévar* and *Manzanilla.*

Huesca

This region has a very varied terrain which includes mountains and plain. The oils produced here are sweet, fruity and yellow. The main olive varieties are *Verdeña, Empeltre* and *Negral.*

Jaén

This is the largest region of olive oil production in Spain. Its mainly mountainous terrain contains 435,000 hectares of olive groves. The oil is mostly blended in modern oil mills which produce a pale yellow oil of good quality. The main variety in this region is *Picual.*

Sierra de Segura, which has its own label of origin, is situated in Jaén. Its olive groves are on rugged, steep-sloped hills covering about 38,000 hectares; the average temperature is 17°C. The main olive variety here is also *Picual.*

Lérida

This region, situated in north-western Spain, has a terrain of hills and valleys. Its Mediterranean climate is ideal for the olive tree because it prevents the temperature from rising too high. The oil produced is of two types: green from the early-picked olives and yellow from the fully ripe fruit. Much of the olive oil from this region is exported to Italy. The main olive varieties grown in Lérida are *Arbequina, Verdeña* and *Verdiell.*

Borjas Blancas, which was the first olive-growing area to be granted its own label of origin, is situated in the southern part of Lérida. Its olive groves cover 35,000 hectares, producing 5,000 tonnes of olive oil per year. Its oil is of the highest quality in Spain. The main varieties in Borjas Blancas are *Arbequina* and *Verdiell.*

Madrid

The main olive varieties cultivated in this region are *Cornicabra* and *Manzanilla.*

Málaga

The olive groves in this region cover 111,000 hectares. The best oils, which are mild-flavoured and yellow, come from the northern area. The main variety is *Hojiblanca.*

Sevilla (Seville)

The oils here are low in acidity and yellow. The main varieties are *Manzanilla, Gordal* and *Verdial.*

Tarragona

There are two large areas of olive oil production in this region: Arbequina and Bajo Ebro. The oil is light, fruity and yellow. The main varieties are *Farga Morruda* and *Servillenca*.

Siurana, which has its own label of origin, is situated in an area running from east to west across Tarragona. The olives are grown at a height of between 200 and 400 metres. The main varieties are *Arbequina, Rojal* and *Morruda*.

Teruel

The olive groves in this region are situated along the Ebro river valley. The climate is continental, with temperatures that are below freezing in winter. The oil is sweet, light and mild. The main variety is *Empeltre*.

Toledo

The olive groves in this region cover about 30,000 hectares. The oils produced are pale yellow and have a low acidity. The main variety is *Cornicabra*.

Valencia

The olive groves in this region cover 30,000 hectares. They produce oils of high quality which are greenish yellow in colour and fruity. The main varieties are *Villalonga, Cornicabra* and *Manzanilla*.

Zaragoza (Saragossa)

This region produces fruity oils of varying quality. The main varieties are *Arbequina* and *Empeltre*.

GREEK OLIVE OIL

Olive oil, like *Feta* cheese and goat's meat, is closely associated with Greek food. It will therefore surprise few people to learn that the Greeks consume more olive oil per capita than any other people in the world. The figure stands at an amazing 23 litres per person per year. This compares with a consumption of only 0.4 litres of olive oil per person per year in France.

Greece is the third-largest producer of olive oil in the world. However, olives are mainly grown on small farms and sent to co-operatives for oil production and export. The average size of olive groves in Greece is 1.8 hectares, producing 500 kilograms of olive oil per year.

The olive has been growing for centuries in the mountainous western region of the country, which is covered with olive groves. More trees are currently being planted, especially on the plains of Greece. These new groves will produce a higher volume of oil per tree, but it will be interesting to taste whether the results are as good in the years to come.

The main olive varieties are *Coroneiki, Throubolia, Valanolia, Mirtolia, Lianolia, Megaritiki, Mastoidis* and *Adramitiki*.

The main growing regions in southern Greece are Kríti (Crete), Pelopónnisos (Peloponnese) and the Aegean islands. In central Greece they are Stylis, Árta, Evia, Ágrinion and the Ionian islands. In northern Greece they are Vólos, Thásos (Thassos) and Khalkidhikí (Chalcidice).

The best oils are produced in Kríti, Lakonikós (Laconia), Messíni (Messina) and Zákinthos (Zante).

FRENCH OLIVE OIL

France is one of the smallest producing countries, but French olive oil is often found on sale in the UK. The average French annual production of olives is only about 2,000 tonnes.

The production areas are in southern and south-eastern France and in Corse (Corsica). The olive groves lie south of a line along the Mediterranean coast running from the Spanish border up to Valence and then across to Menton on the Italian border.

① ALPES-DE-HAUTE-PROVENCE	⑦ GARD
② ALPES-MARITIMES	⑧ HAUTE-CORSE
③ AUDE	⑨ HÉRAULT
④ BOUCHES-DU-RHÔNE	⑩ PYRÉNÉES-ORIENTALES
⑤ CORSE-DU-SUD	⑪ VAR
⑥ DRÔME	⑫ VAUCLUSE

The olive grows in only 12 *départments* of France. These are Alpes-de-Haute-Provence, Alpes-Maritimes, Aude, Bouches-du-Rhône, Corse-du-Sud, Drôme, Gard, Haute-Corse, Hérault, Pyrénées-Orientales, Var and Vaucluse. There are some 200 oil mills and co-operatives, and about 30,000 olive-growers.

The main centres of production are at Nyons and the area around the Vallée des Baux. Other areas which produce high-quality oils are Gard, Vaucluse, Alpes-Maritimes and Corse (Corsica). The main varieties of olive are *La Tanche, Picholine, Grossane* and *Salenenque.*

Nyons

Nyons is in the *départment* of Drôme. It is a small town nestling at the foothills of the Alps on the River Aigues in Provence. It has its own microclimate, ideal for growing the olive. In 1968, it was given its own *Appellation d'Origine.* The main olive variety is *La Tanche.*

La Vallée des Baux

This is in the *départment* of Bouches-du-Rhône, centred around the beautiful fortified hill-town of Les Baux, some 18 miles from Avignon. The Vallée des Baux has a flat terrain, fringed by the hills of Les Alpilles, with Maussane-les-Alpilles as its main town. The area produces an oil of unusually strong and distinctive flavour, which is dark green. The main varieties are *Picholine, Grossane* and *Salenenque.*

TUNISIAN OLIVE OIL

The olive tree has been flourishing in North Africa since Roman times, and Tunisia is the largest African producer of olive oil. Most production is controlled by the Tunisian Olive Oil Board, which monitors the quality of the oil.

There are more than 50 million olive trees in Tunisia, producing an average of about 120,000 tonnes of olive oil a year. Olive oil is very important to the Tunisian economy. More than half of the oil is exported, and 20 per cent of the population is involved in its cultivation and production.

TURKISH OLIVE OIL

The average annual olive oil production in Turkey is 80,000 tonnes, but this figure fluctuates greatly from year to year. In 1983, for example, production was 160,000 tonnes.

The Turkish government has invested a great deal in the liquid vegetable oil industry, including olive oil, and this is one of the most improved sectors of the Turkish food industry. The olive oil industry in Turkey is controlled by agricultural sales co-operatives.

PORTUGUESE OLIVE OIL

Portugal is one of the larger producers of olive oil in the world. It has a mountainous terrain, similar to Greece, and a dry climate which is ideal for producing olive oil. As in most Mediterranean countries, the olive grows in areas where the vine flourishes; one of the best areas is in the Douro Alto, where port is produced.

There are about 50 million olive trees in Portugal – roughly the same number as in Tunisia. However, because of the different climate and terrain, average annual production is only 40,000 tonnes, which is about one-third of Tunisian production.

OTHER OLIVE OIL PRODUCING COUNTRIES

The other important olive oil producing countries are Morocco, Algeria, Syria, Libya, Argentina and Jordan. These account for about seven per cent of world production.

The smaller producing countries are France, the USA, Albania, Cyprus, Lebanon, Yugoslavia, Israel, Iran, Iraq, Brazil, Chile, Peru, Egypt and Mexico. These 14 countries produce about two per cent of the world total.

NUT OILS

These are oils produced only from the crushed nuts of certain trees. A nut is any seed or fruit which consists of an oily kernel within a hard shell. About 95 per cent of nut oils are produced in France, mainly in the walnut-growing areas of the Dordogne. The various types of nut oils are walnut oil, hazelnut oil, almond oil, pineseed oil and pistachio oil.

NUT OIL PRODUCTION

The production of nut oil is fairly simple. The real skill lies in selecting the nuts for production and in the care taken while roasting the pulp.

The selected nuts are either broken manually or by a simple machine and then sorted by hand. Once broken, the nuts are kept at a temperature of 4-5°C to prevent rancidity or spoilage by insects. They are then taken to the mill and placed in a trough with two millstones in it, where they are crushed. The crushed pulp is placed in cauldrons and heated to 160-180°C. The duration of this heat treatment depends on the type of nut being processed. The pulp is constantly stirred to prevent burning. Unroasted nut oils, like coffee beans, have no smell or taste. It is this cooking which gives the oil both taste and aroma.

During the cooking, all of the free oil is run off. The remaining paste is placed on mats rather like olive paste, and it is then subjected to a pressure of 250-300 tonnes. The free-run oil and the pressed oil are mixed and passed into settling tanks, where they are stored for use. The oil is filtered before bottling, and is then ready for use.

Grading nut oils

The quality of nut oils depends on the varieties of the different kinds of nuts used. Top-quality nuts will produce top-quality oil and poor nuts, poor oil.

CULINARY USES

Unroasted nut oils are used in wood-preserving and cosmetics, but roasted nut oils have a number of valuable culinary applications.

Nut oils are primarily used in the kitchen as salad oils. They make interesting dressings and can be used to flavour mayonnaise. Though they are not suitable for deep-frying, they can be used for roasting or grilling meat and for flavouring stir-fry dishes. Walnut and hazelnut oils can be used to give a fried egg quite a different flavour, to toss vegetables such as courgettes or mushrooms over a high heat for a hot salad, to flavour mayonnaise, or to use in place of butter when serving a side dish of beans or leeks.

Because the oils generally taste of the nuts from which they are made, they can also be used in baking to bring out these flavours in biscuits, cakes and teabreads.

Storage

Nut oils are affected by air and light, and they are best kept in a cool place. They should preferably be bought in tins. Unlike olive oil, they do not crystallize. However, they do go opaque if kept at very low temperatures.

WALNUT OIL

Walnut oil has been used for centuries in an unroasted form. In the past, it was made into varnishes and used, for example, on the famous Stradivarius violins. Today it is still used in specialist wood treatments, but it mainly goes into expensive cosmetics. Unroasted walnut oil is very thick; it has no smell and little taste. It is very expensive because, without heating, less oil is extracted.

Walnut oil has only been roasted and exploited for culinary use since the 19th century. The French call it *Huile de Noix*. The oil is topaz in colour and has a distinctive nutty flavour. Two kilos of walnuts are needed to produce one litre of walnut oil.

Physical properties of walnut oil	
Solidification point	Below 0°C
Nutritional values of walnut oil	
Saturated fatty acids: mainly palmitic acid	8-11%
Monounsaturated fatty acids: mainly oleic acid	15-18%
Polyunsaturated fatty acids: mainly linoleic acid	51-62%
linolenic acid	10-19%
Iodine value	132-162

The world's largest producer of walnuts is the USA, followed by Turkey and then Romania. France produces about 350 tonnes of walnut oil per year, of which about 230 tonnes are exported.

There are as many different qualities of walnut oils as there are varieties of walnut, because the quality of the oil depends on the quality of the nut. Producers could import Indian nuts into France, press them and produce a walnut oil from France, but the quality might not be the same as oil produced from French walnuts. Within France there are different qualities – even among nuts off the same tree.

The French have two grades for nuts which are taken off the same tree. The more expensive nut is called *Blanc Extra* and the cheaper nut is called *Arlequin.* They differ both in colour and taste. Walnut buyers use colour as their chief guide in buying. The most expensive walnuts are French, followed by Californian, Turkish, Indian and Chinese.

The walnut tree is native to Asia. It is now grown in south-eastern Europe, west and central Asia, China and North America. There are many different varieties, but the finest walnuts for making oil come from France and the best French walnuts come from the Dordogne. The finest varieties are *La Franquette, La Mayette, La Parisienne, La Marbot, La Corne* and *La Grandjean.*

La Franquette
Originally from the region of Vinay in the Isère, this variety was exported to California in 1870. It is widespread in the nut orchards around Grenoble. The nut, which is large, is harvested in the first fortnight of October.

La Mayette
This variety was introduced from Sicily in the 18th century. The kernels are large with yellow skin and have a very good flavour. It is one of the best nuts from the Isère.

La Parisienne
This variety originated in the Isère. It is smaller than the *Franquette* and the *Mayette,* with a white skin. It is harvested in October, but only gives a good yield every two years.

La Marbot
This walnut is found mainly in the Corrèze in the Lot, though a few trees are also found in the Dordogne. It has a very good flavour and it sells well everywhere.

La Corne
This variety of walnut originated in the Corrèze. It is a little like the *Franquette* with white skin, but it has a hard shell and keeps well.

La Grandjean
This is the nut of the Dordogne and is found particularly around Sarlat and Souillac. It has a white skin and is of superb quality.

HAZELNUT OIL

Hazelnut oil was first produced in 1978 and is, therefore, a relatively new oil. It has a strong penetrating smell and a fine taste. Although hazelnut oil has a similar colour to walnut oil, it is more delicate – strong and yet subtle.

Hazelnuts are harder than walnuts and contain less oil, so 2.5 kilos of nuts are required to produce one litre of oil. The hazelnuts which are used for oil production come from France, Italy and Turkey.

Physical properties of hazelnut oil	
Solidification point	Below 0°C
Nutritional values of hazelnut oil	
Saturated fatty acids: mainly palmitic acid	5-10%
Monounsaturated fatty acids: mainly oleic acid	66-86%
Polyunsaturated fatty acids: mainly linoleic acid	7-24%
linolenic acid	0.1-6%
Iodine value	83-90

ALMOND OIL

Almond oil was first produced in 1980. It takes three kilos of almonds to produce one litre of almond oil. Most of the almonds which are crushed for oil come from Spain and production is centred in France.

Physical properties of almond oil	
Solidification point	Below 0°C
Nutritional values of almond oil	
Saturated fatty acids: mainly palmitic acid	5-10%
Monounsaturated fatty acids: mainly oleic acid	66-86%
Polyunsaturated fatty acids: mainly linoleic acid	7-25%
linolenic acid	trace
Iodine value	92-106

Almond oil goes particularly well with fish. Brush it on grilled plaice or trout towards the end of the cooking time, or bake in foil in the oven. Use it with wine vinegar as a dressing for avocados, or use it to fry flaked almonds and toss over cooked cauliflower or broccoli.

Amande douce

Amande douce is an oil that is mainly used in the pharmaceutical and cosmetic industries. It is made in the same way as almond oil but no heat is used to extract the flavour and smell. This oil has little taste and is often labelled as plain almond oil.

PINESEED OIL

Pineseed oil was first produced in 1984. It is an extremely expensive oil as many kilos of pinenuts are needed to produce a small quantity of oil. The taste and flavour are very strong indeed and the oil should be used sparingly. The nuts which are crushed for oil come from Spain.

Information concerning the physical properties and nutritional values of pineseed oil is not available.

PISTACHIO OIL

Pistachio is a new oil, which was first produced in 1988. It has a dark green colour and a distinctive smell and taste. The nuts which are crushed for oil come from Iran.

Physical properties of pistachio oil	
Solidification point	Below 0°C
Nutritional values of pistachio oil	
Saturated fatty acids: mainly palmitic acid	8%
Monounsaturated fatty acids: mainly oleic acid	69%
Polyunsaturated fatty acids: mainly linoleic acid	20%
Iodine value	85-98

VEGETABLE OILS

These are oils derived from the seeds of many different plants which grow all over the world. Many plants have oil seeds, but only a few of them have commercial uses. The edible oils should be distinguished from drying oils such as linseed oil and the essential oils used in perfumery. A high proportion of the plants which produce edible oils grow in the tropics.

The various types of vegetable oils are soya oil, rapeseed oil, sunflower oil, palm oil, cottonseed oil, ground-nut oil, coconut oil, corn oil, sesame oil, safflower oil, grapeseed oil, mustard oil, pumpkinseed oil and avocado oil. Unlike nut oils, many of these oils are bought and sold in large quantities on the international commodity market. They are therefore known as commodity oils.

VEGETABLE OIL PRODUCTION

Oil is obtained from the cells of plant seeds, which are normally very small. The oil is either squeezed out of the seeds or dissolved out by means of a solvent. Sometimes, these two basic methods are combined.

Cleaning, breaking and cooking

The seeds are first cleaned to extract chaff, stones and other unwanted scraps. They are then broken up by rollers. This process helps the heat to penetrate during cooking. The cracked seeds are heated in large kettles, usually by steam. The temperature reaches about 70-110°C, depending on the type of seed used in production. This process bursts the walls of the oil cells.

Expelling

Next the seeds go to the expeller: this is a type of screw-press. The oil runs free from this press and is then filtered

VEGETABLE OIL PRODUCING COUNTRIES OF THE WORLD

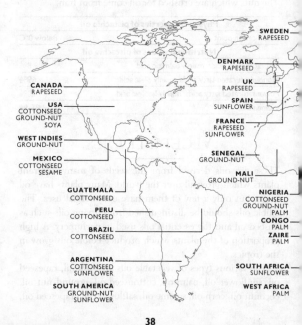

SWEDEN — RAPESEED

DENMARK — RAPESEED

UK — RAPESEED

CANADA — RAPESEED

SPAIN — SUNFLOWER

USA — COTTONSEED GROUND-NUT SOYA

FRANCE — RAPESEED SUNFLOWER

WEST INDIES — GROUND-NUT

SENEGAL — GROUND-NUT

MEXICO — COTTONSEED SESAME

MALI — GROUND-NUT

GUATEMALA — COTTONSEED

NIGERIA — COTTONSEED GROUND-NUT PALM

PERU — COTTONSEED

CONGO — PALM

BRAZIL — COTTONSEED

ZAIRE — PALM

ARGENTINA — COTTONSEED SUNFLOWER

SOUTH AFRICA — SUNFLOWER

SOUTH AMERICA — GROUND-NUT SUNFLOWER

WEST AFRICA — PALM

and stored. At this stage, a small quantity of certain oils, such as sunflower and safflower oil, is bottled and sold. These oils have a much better colour and flavour than most blended oils and they are therefore more expensive.

Solvent extraction

This process removes all remaining oil from the seed cake after expelling. The seed cake is broken up by rollers and flattened. It is then soaked with solvents until almost all the oil has dissolved. The resulting mixture of solvent and oil is pumped to a distilling plant where heat causes the solvent to evaporate. The crude oil is then sent for refining.

Refining

There are three stages in the refining process: removing the natural acid, lightening the colour, and neutralizing the taste and smell.

As a result of the earlier production processes, the chemical structure of the oil has been changed and the oil is now acidic. An alkali, such as caustic soda, is mixed with the oil to remove the acids. The mixture reacts to form a soap, which sinks to the bottom of the tank. The oil is then racked off and washed several times with hot water to make sure that all the soap is removed.

Next, the oil is bleached to lighten the colour, using a fining agent like carbon or Fuller's earth. Everything is

EASTERN EUROPE
RAPESEED
SUNFLOWER

POLAND
RAPESEED

USSR
COTTONSEED
SUNFLOWER

INDIA
COCONUT
GROUND-NUT
RAPESEED
SESAME
SUNFLOWER

CHINA
COTTONSEED
GROUND-NUT
RAPESEED
SESAME
SOYA
SUNFLOWER

JAPAN
SOYA

SRI LANKA
COCONUT

KOREA
SOYA

PHILIPPINES
COCONUT

PAKISTAN
RAPESEED

MALAYSIA
COCONUT
PALM

IRAN
COTTONSEED

INDONESIA
COCONUT
PALM

AUSTRALIA
SUNFLOWER

OCEANIA
PALM
SESAME
COCONUT

AFRICA
PALM
SESAME

mixed together and then the oil is filtered off. The taste and smell are neutralized by passing steam through the hot oil in a vacuum. Unwanted tastes and smells are carried off in the vapour. The resultant oil is completely neutral. It is mixed with some of the first-run oil from the expeller to give it flavour and colour.

WORLD PRODUCTION FIGURES FOR PRINCIPAL COMMODITY OILS, 1987/88 (Figures are in thousand tonnes.)			
Soya oil	15,263	Cottonseed oil	3,401
Rapeseed oil	7,542	Ground-nut oil	3,306
Sunflower oil	7,156	Coconut oil	2,675
Palm oil	5,965	Corn oil	1,127

CULINARY USES

The vast majority of oils used in cooking are vegetable oils. They are used in all culinary applications, both hot and cold, as well as in the manufacture of margarine, in baking and in ready-made convenience dishes. The main advantage of vegetable oils to manufacturers is that, unlike nut oils which are valued for their flavour, they are relatively tasteless. In home cooking, they can always be made more interesting by the addition of olive and nut oils as flavourings. Most vegetable oils have a high smoke point and are thus especially suitable for frying.

Until recently, most oils were blended and sold simply as vegetable oil. However, there has been growing awareness of the varying fatty acid compositions of different oils. As a result, producers have started to market particular types of vegetable oil in an unblended state. Corn oil was one of the first unblended oils to appear on sale in the USA and the UK; it has been closely followed onto the market by sunflower and safflower oils.

Storage

Heat, light and air are bad for all oils. So remember to keep all vegetable oils, including olive and nut oils, firmly sealed in a cool, dark place.

SOYA OIL

Soya oil is produced from the fruit of the soya plant, which is believed to have originated in Asia. The soya plant has grown there since ancient times, and it is still an important food legume in China, Korea, Japan and Malaysia. In recent years, the soya bean has become one of the world's leading sources of vegetable oil, as well as an important source of food in its own right.

Physical properties of soya oil	
Solidification point	Below 0°C
Smoke point	210°C
Nutritional values of soya oil	
Saturated fatty acids	12-16%
Monounsaturated fatty acids: mainly oleic acid	17-57%
Polyunsaturated fatty acids: mainly linoleic acid	28-57%
linolenic acid	at least 2%
Iodine value	103-136

Cultivation and production

The soya bean belongs to the pea family and is a leguminous plant or pulse. There are hundreds of different varieties of soya bean. Increased planting in the USA in recent decades has made the United States the world's main soya oil producer. Soya oil accounts for 42 per cent of the total vegetable oil market.

Culinary uses

Soya oil has important industrial uses in the manufacture of soap, paints, plastics, printing inks, insecticides and paper coatings. Its main culinary usage is in the production of margarine. Soya oil can also be used in the home for frying or basting and for salad dressings.

RAPESEED OIL

Rapeseed oil is also known as coleseed oil. Rape belongs to the wallflower family and is a member of the *Brassica* genus. The seed has an oil content of about 42 per cent; about 2.25 kilos of seed produce one litre of oil.

Physical properties of rapeseed oil	
Solidification point	Below 0°C
Smoke point	225°C
Nutritional values of rapeseed oil	
Saturated fatty acids	6%
Monounsaturated fatty acids: mainly oleic acid	50-60%
Polyunsaturated fatty acids: mainly linoleic acid	12-20%
linolenic acid	at least 8%
Vitamin content	vitamin E
Iodine value	110-115

Cultivation and production

There has been increasing cultivation of rape in the UK. Twenty years ago, rape crops were hardly ever seen; when they were, they were often mistaken for mustard. Now, fields of yellow rape are a common sight in the countryside during the spring.

Throughout Europe the oil-crushing industry, which used to crush soya, is now encouraged by the EEC to crush rapeseed from the new varieties of the plant with a low erucic acid content. There is an EEC-guaranteed minimum selling price, which has resulted in the planting of vast acreages all over Europe. This, in turn, has had the effect of reducing imports and rapeseed oil is now normally the cheapest liquid vegetable oil on the market.

The seeds are cleaned, sorted and then crushed in a continuous screw-press. They are heated to about 100°C and the resultant oil is placed in a centrifuge to eliminate the solid matter. This produces a bright clear oil. A further 15-20 per cent of oil may be obtained by refining the oil cake.

The principal areas of production are India, China, Canada, eastern Europe and France.

Culinary uses

Rapeseed oil is bland and odourless. Its main culinary application is in blends of vegetable oil.

SUNFLOWER OIL

Sunflower oil is the most commonly-sold vegetable oil for household use in the world. The oil content of the sunflower seed is 20-32 per cent and new strains can produce as much as 40 per cent. It takes about two kilos of seeds to produce one litre of oil.

Physical properties of sunflower oil	
Solidification point	Below 0°C
Smoke point	200°C
Nutritional values of sunflower oil	
Saturated fatty acids	10-12%
Monounsaturated fatty acids: mainly oleic acid	14-43%
Polyunsaturated fatty acids: mainly linoleic acid	44-75%
linolenic acid	trace
Iodine value	115-136

Cultivation and production

The sunflower is native to North America and is grown chiefly in temperate climates. It is now cultivated in the USSR, China, South America, southern and central Europe, India and Australia. The USSR and eastern Europe are the largest producers of sunflower oil.

Culinary uses

Sunflower oil is used extensively in the production of cooking fats and in margarine. It is also important as a salad oil. In France, 40 per cent of all vegetable oil consumed is sunflower oil.

PALM OIL

This is one of the most important vegetable oils. Two kinds of oil are obtained from the palm: one from the thick fibrous layer on the outside of the fruit and another from the kernel inside.

Physical properties	Palm oil	Palm kernel oil
Solidification point	38-45°C	24-26°C
Nutritional values	**Palm oil**	**Palm kernel oil**
Saturated fatty acids: mainly lauric acid	45-55%	56-63%
Monounsaturated fatty acids: mainly oleic acid	38-50%	10-17%
Polyunsaturated fatty acids: mainly linoleic acid	6-11%	15-21%
Iodine value	46-60	16-23

Cultivation and production

The palm is indigenous to West Africa. It is cultivated some five degrees north and south of the equator in Africa, in the Congo and Nigeria, and also in Malaysia and Indonesia. Palm trees require hot, humid conditions and a high rainfall. The palm is an important and successful crop in these regions as it will grow on poor soil.

Palm oil taken from the thick fibrous layer around the fruit is yellow or reddish orange before refining. Palm kernel oil is white or light yellow.

Culinary uses

Both palm oil and palm kernel oil are used as cooking oils. Palm oil is used in the production of margarine and in the baking industry for biscuits and other foods. It is also used extensively in the UK in fish and chip shops. The oil is relatively cheap and it is tasteless; animal fats like lard are added to give flavour.

COTTONSEED OIL

The cotton plant is, of course, grown primarily to produce cotton fibre for the manufacture of clothes and other cotton products; cottonseed is a by-product. The oil content of the seed varies between 15 and 25 per cent. Cottonseed oil is a clear yellow colour, with no taste or smell.

Physical properties of cottonseed oil	
Smoke point	220°C
Nutritional values of cottonseed oil	
Saturated fatty acids	23-28%
Monounsaturated fatty acids	22-28%
Polyunsaturated fatty acids	44-53%
Iodine value	99-119

Cultivation and production

The cotton plant is grown in tropical, sub-tropical and warm temperate climates. The main producers are the USSR, the USA and China. The plant produces flowers which are red, pink or cream in colour. When the flowers mature, the plant produces a seed which is surrounded by white fluffy fibres. The fibres and seeds are separated in a gin, and oil is extracted from the seeds using solvents. The unrefined oil is dark reddish brown and needs considerable refining for culinary use.

Culinary uses

Culinary uses for cottonseed were not discovered until the late 19th century. Today, cottonseed oil is widely used in the manufacture of margarine, cooking oils and dressings.

GROUND-NUT OIL

The ground-nut is also known as the monkey-nut, the peanut, the earth-nut and the Arachis nut – but it is actually a pulse, not a nut. The oil produced from it is sometimes known as peanut oil or Arachis oil, and is an important commodity oil.

Physical properties of ground-nut oil	
Solidification point	Below 0°C
Smoke point	210°C
Nutritional values of ground-nut oil	
Saturated fatty acids	6-8%
Monounsaturated fatty acids: mainly oleic acid	37-70%
Polyunsaturated fatty acids: mainly linoleic acid	14-45%
linolenic acid	less than 0.5%
Vitamin content	vitamins B and E
Iodine value	83-105

Cultivation and production

The ground-nut is a native of South America and the West Indies. It is cultivated in most tropical and sub-tropical regions of the world, and in the USA as far north as Virginia. It is an annual propagated by seed, with a crop period of four to five months. The nuts contain 30 per cent protein and 40-50 per cent oil. The largest producers are India, China, Nigeria and the USA.

Culinary uses

Ground-nut oil is widely used as a blending oil because it is almost tasteless. As such, it brings out the flavour of food in cooking without affecting the taste itself. It is also particularly useful for making mayonnaise and other dressings, as it lends itself easily to forming an emulsion.

COCONUT OIL

Coconut oil is extracted from the dried kernel of the coconut, or *copra*, which is the white flesh of the fresh nut. The oil changes from a solid to a liquid form much faster than most other vegetable oils; this is because of the high percentage of saturated fat contained in it.

Physical properties of coconut oil	
Solidification point	21-23°C
Nutritional values of coconut oil	
Saturated fatty acids: mainly lauric, myristic and palmitic acids	90%
Monounsaturated fatty acids: mainly oleic acid	7.5%
Polyunsaturated fatty acids: mainly linoleic acid	2.5% or less
Iodine value	7-10

Cultivation and production

The coconut palm grows in the tropics and is of unknown origin. The chief areas of production for the oil are the Philippines, the Pacific islands, Indonesia and India. *Copra* yields about 60 per cent oil.

Culinary uses

Coconut oil is used locally in the producing countries as a cooking oil. Commercially it is used in the manufacture of cooking oils, fats and margarine.

CORN OIL

Corn oil, which is extracted from corn or maize, is a by-product in the manufacture of starch. About two kilos of corn germ produce one litre of oil. The crude oil is reddish amber and corn oil remains darker than most other vegetable oils after refining. It is promoted in the West as an oil high in polyunsaturates and low in saturated fats.

Physical properties of corn oil	
Solidification point	Below 0°C
Smoke point	210°C
Nutritional values of corn oil	
Saturated fatty acids	10-12%
Monounsaturated fatty acids: mainly oleic acid	43%
Polyunsaturated fatty acids: mainly linoleic acid	42-45%
linolenic acid	trace
Iodine value	110-130

Cultivation and production

Corn is one of the principal crops grown in North America, and the USA produces some 70 per cent of the world's corn oil. Along with rapeseed oil, it is one of the cheapest vegetable oils on the market.

Culinary uses

Corn oil can be used for most kinds of cooking. It is widely used in the manufacture of margarine and baked foods.

SESAME OIL

There are two types of sesame oil. One is processed in the normal way to produce an oil which is yellowish green in colour; it has a strong pleasing flavour and aroma. The other uses roasted seeds to produce a dark oil which varies from brown to black in colour and has an extremely strong taste and smell. Sesame seeds contain 45-55 per cent oil.

Physical properties of sesame oil	
Solidification point	Below 0°C
Nutritional values of sesame oil	
Saturated fatty acids: mainly palmitic acid	7-9%
Monounsaturated fatty acids: mainly oleic acid	45-46%
Polyunsaturated fatty acids: mainly linoleic acid	35-41%
Iodine value	100-113

Cultivation and production

Sesame is an annual plant which takes between three and five months to mature. It originated in Africa, but has been grown for centuries in India and China, and is now common in most tropical and sub-tropical areas of the world. Today, the largest producing regions are India, China and Africa.

Culinary uses

Sesame oil is used in cooking and as a salad oil. Roasted sesame oil is much favoured in Chinese cooking. A few drops will give any dish a strong flavour of sesame.

SAFFLOWER OIL

Originating in India, the safflower has been grown for centuries, both for the dye from its petals and for its oil, which was used for burning in lamps. The oil content of the seed varies between 25 and 37 per cent. The crude oil is dark red and needs considerable refining to achieve an acceptable colour.

Physical properties of safflower oil	
Solidification point	Below 0°C
Nutritional values of safflower oil	
Saturated fatty acids: mainly palmitic acid	6-9%
Monounsaturated fatty acids: mainly oleic acid	16-29%
Polyunsaturated fatty acids: mainly linoleic acid	63-72%
linolenic acid	0.1-6%
Iodine value	129-151

Cultivation and production

The safflower thrives on semi-arid land, and it is now grown in a number of countries which have a hot climate and a light dry soil. The oil is obtained by pressing the seed and by solvent extraction. Most safflower oil is produced in the USA; other important producing countries are India, Mexico, Spain, Portugal and Australia.

Culinary uses

Safflower is now gaining in commercial importance as an oilseed. In the Western world, culinary interest in safflower oil has grown with the demand for oils which are high in polyunsaturates.

GRAPESEED OIL

Grapeseed oil was invented in the South of France during the First World War and further developed after the Second World War. It has the highest linoleic fatty acid content of any culinary oil.

Physical properties of grapeseed oil	
Solidification point	Below 0°C
Smoke point	230°C
Nutritional values of grapeseed oil	
Saturated fatty acids	7-8%
Monounsaturated fatty acids	trace
Polyunsaturated fatty acids: mainly linoleic acid	72-75%
linolenic acid	0.35%
Iodine value	140-150

Production

The production of grapeseed oil is concentrated on the vast areas of vineyards in the South of France, where there is no shortage of grapes. In 1984, 20,000 tonnes of oil were produced for sale worldwide.

Culinary uses

Because of its high smoke point, grapeseed oil is particularly useful for deep-frying and for *fondue*. It can also be used in salad dressings and mayonnaise.

MUSTARD OIL

Mustard oil can be obtained from both black and brown mustard seed (see pages 59-61 for further information on mustard seed). In India, mustard oil is used in the same way as *ghee*. It is also used in commercial salad creams and in soaps, lubricants and lighting fuels.

Mustard oil has a distinctive smell and a soft, light flavour with a little heat in the taste. It contains a very high level of erucic acid, which is thought by Western experts to have a detrimental effect on the body.

Physical properties of mustard oil	
Solidification point	Below 0°C
Nutritional values of mustard oil	
Saturated fatty acids: mainly palmitic acid	0.2%
Monounsaturated fatty acids: mainly oleic and erucic acids	65-83%
Polyunsaturated fatty acids: mainly linoleic acid	18-20%
linolenic acid	2-3%
Iodine value	93-124

PUMPKINSEED OIL

Crude pumpkinseed oil is a reddish brown and needs heavy refining to achieve an acceptable yellow colour. It has little smell and a sweetish taste.

Physical properties of pumpkinseed oil	
Solidification point	Below 0°C
Nutritional values of pumpkinseed oil	
Saturated fatty acids: mainly palmitic acid	12%
Monounsaturated fatty acids: mainly oleic acid	35%
Polyunsaturated fatty acids: mainly linoleic acid	35-45%
Iodine value	119-131

AVOCADO OIL

This is a new oil produced from avocados grown along the coastal mountain ranges of southern California. It is produced without chemical solvents by a simple process of adding water to the fruit, crushing the mixture to a paste and then placing the paste in a centrifuge.

Avocado oil is golden yellow and has a light aniseed smell and flavour. It is a mainly monounsaturated oil and is claimed, by the producers, to contain fewer calories than other oils. It is difficult to obtain in Europe.

Physical properties of avocado oil	
Smoke point	220°C
Nutritional values of avocado oil	
Saturated fatty acids	10%
Monounsaturated fatty acids	80%
Polyunsaturated fatty acids	3%
Vitamin content	vitamin E

VINEGARS

INTRODUCTION

Vinegar is a medieval word which means literally "sour wine". There are many definitions of vinegar, but it may be broadly defined as a liquid consisting of dilute acetic acid.

The various types of vinegars are wine vinegars, spirit vinegar, grain vinegars (including malt vinegar), cider vinegar and non-brewed condiment. In Europe and the USA non-brewed condiment, which is made from chemically produced acetic acid, may not legally be marketed under the label "vinegar".

VINEGAR PRODUCTION

Vinegar is obtained by double fermentation. The first fermentation converts the sugar in liquids such as grape juice or malt wort into alcohol; the second converts the resultant alcoholic liquid into vinegar by acetous fermentation. The level of acetic acid varies depending on the type of vinegar produced.

Acetous fermentation results from the action of the bacterium *Acetobacter xylinum*. This bacterium occurs naturally in wine-growing areas, and the first vinegar was probably made accidentally by leaving wine out in the hot sun. Today, most vinegar is produced from pure strains of cultivated bacteria in a controlled acetator. (See wine vinegar production, pages 50-52.)

Vinegar can be made anywhere in the world. However, most wine vinegars are made in wine-producing regions. In the same way, grain vinegars are usually manufactured in the large grain-producing countries.

COOKING WITH VINEGAR

Vinegar has a variety of different uses in the kitchen. Its principal application is in salad dressings and mayonnaise. The best-quality vinegars produce the best results. For example, anyone who finds the taste of malt vinegar a little too sharp should try a good wine or cider vinegar; the difference is substantial.

Vinegar is also an important ingredient for making pickles and chutneys. Here the choice of vinegar will depend on the strength of acidity and flavour, and on the colour required in the finished pickle.

In general cooking, vinegar may be used to deglaze after frying or roasting and to add flavour to sauces or gravies. It may also be added to "barbecue" recipes, casseroles and marinades. A little vinegar added to the cooking water helps eggs to retain their shape during poaching.

It is essential to use the right kind of equipment when cooking with vinegar. The acid content of certain vinegars may attack pans or lids, and this interaction may also affect the food being cooked.

Storing vinegar

Vinegar can be stored at room temperature. Keep it in a well-stoppered container away from the light. Flavoured vinegars, in particular, lose their taste with age.

Commercial uses for vinegar

As more and more consumers question the use of artificial preservatives in food, a growing number of food manufacturers are turning to natural preservatives like vinegar. Vinegar helps to prevent the growth of micro-organisms and it is a more effective food preservative than acetic acid in its pure form.

Bakers were one of the first groups of food producers to replace the preservative E283 in their products with a small quantity of vinegar. The quantities of vinegar used are not large enough to preserve food products over a long period, but they will, nevertheless, keep them fresher than if no vinegar had been added.

WINE VINEGARS

In Germany and Austria, wine vinegar is defined as a liquid which contains five per cent of water-free acetic acid obtained by acetous fermentation. In France and the UK, the acetic acid level must be six per cent. However, in the UK, the acidity level does not have to be stated on the label; in France, this is obligatory. In Spain and Portugal, wine vinegar is the only form of vinegar allowed.

WINE VINEGAR PRODUCTION

Wine vinegar is made wherever wine is produced. In the past, vineyard owners would simply leave a half-empty cask of wine out in the heat of the sun; after some months, bacteria in the air would usually have turned it into vinegar.

Another traditional method of making vinegar is to use wooden vats filled with small coils of a wood such as birch, which are impregnated with *Acetobacter*. The wine is pumped into the top of the vat and allowed to trickle to the bottom. From there it is pumped up to the top again. When all the liquid has been converted by the bacteria into vinegar, it is drained off. The culture of *Acetobacter* remains in the coils of birch wood so that when new wine is pumped into the same vat the process starts all over again.

Modern methods of production

The most modern and indeed the quickest way to make wine vinegar is to use an acetator. Here the wine to be converted into vinegar is placed in a large 30,000-litre vat. A specially bred starter-culture of vinegar-producing bacteria is added and then warm air is filtered through the wine to raise its temperature to 30°C. This is the optimum temperature for converting wine to vinegar; even a 15 second gap in the supply of warm air will cause the vinegar culture to die.

The conversion of all the wine to vinegar takes about 15 days. Roughly speaking, a wine which has 11 degrees of alcohol will produce a vinegar with 11 degrees of acetic acid. The alcohol content of the finished wine vinegar, however, will be around 0.5 per cent.

Storing, filtering and bottling

Raw vinegar is cloudy because of the acetic acid bacteria, and it needs special filtration. It is also unstable as it contains certain dissolved substances which can suddenly become insoluble. For this reason, the raw vinegar is stored for a while so that any insoluble matter precipitates. This problem is much more acute with red wine vinegar than white. When vinegar is stored the quality of the taste and the aroma improve.

After the vinegar has been made it is normally fined with bentonite to clear most of the bacteria. This makes the liquid easier to filter. The old method of filtration was to pass the vinegar through filters filled with a special powdered earth. The new method is to use a continuous stream filter such as a Frings filter. This method, whereby the vinegar is passed through the walls of a filter module, is efficient and self-cleaning.

When the vinegar is ready to bottle, water must be added to it in order to bring down the strength of the acetic acid. Vinegar has a preserving property, but in itself it is very unstable. One of the ways round this problem is to pasteurize it. The pasteurization kills off the enzymes and micro-organisms. This is done by heating the vinegar to about 75 °C for 40 seconds. The temperature and time may vary, depending on the vinegar, but care must be taken as this process can change the taste, smell and colour of the vinegar. Sulphur may also be added to stabilize the vinegar, but this is illegal in certain countries such as France.

When the vinegar is ready for bottling, it may be sterile-filtered just as a final precaution and is then sealed. It is essential that air does not get in as this may cause spoilage.

Analysis of a typical wine vinegar	
(Figures are based on a Bordeaux wine vinegar of 7 degrees acidity.)	
Total acidity	7%
Volatile acidity	6.9%
Acetic acid	6.8%
Tartaric acid	1515 mg per litre
Lactic acid	280 mg per litre
Succinic acid	315 mg per litre
Citric acid	traces

CULINARY USES

Wine vinegar on its own or vinegar and stock are excellent for deglazing frying or roasting pans; this provides a first-class sauce for the food which has been cooked in them. Use a high-quality wine vinegar or flavoured vinegar. Tarragon vinegar is excellent with chicken; raspberry vinegar goes well with venison or wild boar, as well as with chicken; and sherry vinegar is good with all red meats. Fish, too, can be treated in this way. Try mackerel with raspberry vinegar and fresh herbs. Add the vinegar and herbs to the pan when the fish is cooked. Remove the fish to fillet and finish off the sauce with cream.

Wine vinegar can be added to stews and casseroles. Sherry vinegar is especially good used in this way. It can also be used to enhance tomato juice and tomato sauces, or added to tomato soup just before serving.

WHITE WINE VINEGAR

The quality of all wine vinegars depends upon the quality of wine used. Any white wine may be used as long as it is checked first for flavour and taste. White wine is the base for most flavoured vinegars.

CHAMPAGNE VINEGAR

Champagne vinegar should be made from wine produced during the manufacture of champagne, at the degorgement stage when the sediment is removed from the bottle by freezing. The ice-plug can be thawed and used to make vinegar after the wine has been filtered.

RED WINE VINEGAR

This vinegar is made in the same way as other wine vinegars, but it is often stored in wood rather than stainless steel. If the vinegar is stored for six months or more it may be called aged wine vinegar. Red wine vinegar has a much fuller flavour than white wine vinegar.

Bordeaux vinegar

This is a red wine vinegar made from wine that has an *Appellation Bordeaux Contrôllée*.

SHERRY VINEGAR

Sherry vinegar is made in oak sherry casks by the traditional method. There are two types of sherries produced in Jerez: one that grows a form of yeast called *flor* on it and one that does not. The wine without *flor,* which is called Raya, is used in the production of the Oloroso sherry; it is this wine that is used to make sherry vinegar.

The Raya is poured into a cask until the cask is half-full. It is then placed out in the full heat of the sun and the wine turns naturally to vinegar. It produces a strong, pungent flavour while still retaining the taste of sherry. Sherry vinegar can be either light or dark in colour.

RASPBERRY VINEGAR

Raspberries are added to white wine vinegar and allowed to macerate for about a month. At the end of this time the vinegar is filtered off and bottled. The vinegar is now red and has a wonderful aroma of fresh raspberries.

TARRAGON VINEGAR

Fresh tarragon is added to white wine vinegar. After a few days the vinegar will taste and smell of tarragon. It is extremely important that the tarragon used is of the French variety. Russian tarragon, which looks the same and costs much less, is useless because it has no taste.

BALSAMIC VINEGAR

In the space of a few years, this vinegar has become very fashionable among the smart restaurants of London and New York; yet the majority of people know very little about it. It comes from Modena and the surrounding area in Italy. The centre of production is at Spilamberto, some 16 kilometres from Modena. Balsamic vinegar has been made for centuries on Italian farms by noble families for their own consumption. Before 1966, when it first became commercially available, the only way to obtain a bottle was to be given one as a present.

Traditional methods of production

The production of balsamic vinegar is much more complicated than that of other vinegars. It is made from the reduced must of grapes added to vinegar. This mixture is then stored for a long time in wooden barrels.

The first stage is must production. The main grape variety used to prepare the must is *Trebbiano*. Other varieties used are *Ancellotta, Spergola, Ciocchella, Occhio di gatta* and *Pellegrina*. To produce a good must the grapes should be mature and possess the correct ratio between sugar and acidity. The freshly-pressed must is placed in a copper cauldron over an open fire and heated to 60-80°C. This kills the yeasts, which otherwise would start a fermentation, and sterilizes the must; artificial preservatives cannot be used to kill the yeasts as this would produce an unpleasant taste and smell. The boiling process is continued in order to concentrate the must and reduce the volume. This increases the sugar content to around 14-18 degrees Baume and reduces the must by about one-third. It is then cooled. If a mould forms on top of the must the whole boiling process has to start again to kill it. For this reason it is important that all the equipment is kept scrupulously clean.

The second stage of production is acetous fermentation. Five or six wooden casks are thoroughly cleaned with boiling vinegar. Into each cask is put some good-quality vinegar and a vinegar mother, which looks rather like a piece of fresh liver. The barrels are then filled nearly to the top with the must. After a few years the liquid has all been transformed into vinegar. Every five or six years the vinegar mother is extracted and used for making more vinegar. The casks are sometimes brought into the sunlight to accelerate the acetous fermentation. The barrels used in this process are made of various woods such as chestnut, cherry, juniper, mulberry, oak and ash – each of which impregnates the vinegar with its own special flavour.

The final stage of production is maturation and ageing. As the vinegar matures and ages, it is transferred to smaller casks which may hold anything from ten to 75 litres. Every year the vinegar is moved from one cask to another. The really old vinegars have a thick consistency and may have been kept for over a hundred years.

Industrial methods of production

In 1966, a competition was held at San Giovanni in Spilamberto to find the best balsamic vinegar. This provided the publicity for a new interest in the vinegar and the whole business snowballed. A consortium was started called *Consorteria dell'Aceto Balsamico* which now holds regular courses for the establishment of vinegar factories; it also holds courses on the important issues of taste and aroma in an attempt to maintain quality.

Factory-produced balsamic vinegar is made by boiling the must rapidly in stainless steel vats and using a much faster ageing process. Because of rapid expansion in production after 1966, the quality began to suffer, but the consortium is trying to correct this.

Good-quality balsamic vinegar is dark brown to black; its taste is fruity and sweet, but with a balance of acidity and a fine aromatic smell. Some commercial brands, however, which have not aged sufficiently, are just dark, sweet liquids. It is usually better to buy balsamic vinegar made by small producers if you can find it.

HOME-MADE WINE VINEGAR

It is fairly simple to make wine vinegar at home. All that is needed is a stone crock, a vinegar mother and some wine. Place the wine and vinegar mother in the stone crock and after a few days the wine will have started to change into vinegar. It is best to place the crock in a warm place such as the kitchen. The vinegar mother should never touch any metal object as this will kill it, so only use wooden spoons when handling the mother.

FLAVOURED VINEGARS

Flavoured vinegars are made in a variety of different ways, but their purpose is that they should taste of the added ingredients; too often it is debatable whether this is so.

A fine flavour and aroma can be achieved by producing vinegar from good wine, using fresh herbs and spices. However, this method is expensive and there are ways of cutting costs. Take, for example, a bottle of raspberry vinegar which has the words "natural ingredients" on the label. Red wine vinegar will have been used to provide the colour; a natural essence, rather than fresh raspberries, may have been added for taste or smell. For good measure, the manufacturer might even drop a couple of raspberries into each bottle. The result can be appalling if too much essence is added. When the essence is carefully used, flavoured vinegars can have a good taste: the chemicals used are the same as those which occur naturally in the fruit. But it would help if they were labelled accordingly.

Here is a list of flavoured vinegars which may be found in delicatessens and specialist shops:

Bilberry vinegar	Herb vinegar	Peach vinegar
Blackcurrant vinegar	Honey vinegar	Raspberry vinegar
Cherry vinegar	Lemon vinegar	Redcurrant vinegar
Dill vinegar	Mint vinegar	Sage vinegar
Garlic vinegar	Nutmeg vinegar	Shallot vinegar
Green pepper vinegar	Oregano vinegar	Thyme vinegar

GRAIN VINEGARS

Grain vinegars may be colourless ("white vinegar") or light to dark brown. They have a strong, sharp flavour with acidity levels that vary from four to six per cent of acetic acid. They include malt vinegar, brown malt vinegar, distilled malt vinegar and rice vinegar.

MALT VINEGAR

Malt vinegar is made in three stages. First the grain arrives at the factory and is fed into large cookers filled with water and heated by steam. The starch in the grain forms a solution in the water. Barley malt is added to convert the insoluble starch into sugar. The liquid or wort is then pumped off the grain and transferred to vats.

During the second stage of the process, yeast is added to the wort. This converts the sugar into alcohol, producing a liquid of about six or seven per cent alcohol. The alcoholic fermentation takes three to four days. After this period, the alcoholic liquor is put into vats which contain birch chippings similar to those used for wine vinegar production, or into an acetator to convert the alcohol to acetic acid. Finally, the resulting vinegar is stored, filtered and bottled.

This kind of malt vinegar is sometimes called light brown vinegar, to distinguish it from brown malt vinegar.

BROWN MALT VINEGAR

This is made in the same way as light brown malt vinegar, but caramel is added during the final process.

DISTILLED MALT VINEGAR

This is obtained by distilling the alcoholic liquor produced at the second stage of the vinegar-making process. Distilled malt vinegar is colourless and therefore especially useful as an additive in the food industry, where it is important to maintain the original colour of the product.

RICE VINEGAR

This is made in the same way as malt vinegar, except that rice is the grain used in the production process.

Cider apples

OTHER VINEGARS

CIDER VINEGAR

Cider vinegar is produced from the juice of apples, which is naturally sweet. To this is added a yeast which converts the sugar into alcohol. The alcohol is then converted into vinegar in the usual way.

Cider vinegar has a low percentage of alcohol. Its percentage of acidity is also lower than other vinegars, at about four to five per cent.

SPIRIT VINEGAR

Spirit vinegar is produced by acetous fermentation from distilled alcohol of agricultural origin. The alcohol is either distilled out of malted grain or, in Europe, from the EEC wine lake. It is made into vinegar in exactly the same way as wine is turned into vinegar.

Spirit vinegar is cheap to produce and has little flavour. It is easy to store because it does not deteriorate when exposed to the air. It is used mainly for pickling.

NON-BREWED CONDIMENT
Until 1950, this liquid was called non-brewed vinegar. However, the word vinegar may no longer be used as a legal label for it. The ingredients speak for themselves: they are water, acetic acid and caramel. Non-brewed condiment is, of course, very cheap. It is mainly used in fish and chip shops in the UK.

SEASONINGS

INTRODUCTION

The word seasoning is often used to mean simply salt and pepper. But there are all kinds of other seasonings which help to bring out the natural flavours of food and add interest, contrast and piquancy.

Most of these flavourings are used in relatively small proportions, but they can make all the difference to a finished dish. Some of them consist of fresh plants as in the case of herbs, garlic and horseradish; others are preserved or manufactured foods like spices, mustards and vegetable pastes. They all offer a wonderful opportunity for experimenting with unusual tastes and flavours in cooking.

MUSTARD

Mustard is one of the oldest known seasonings and also one of the most widely used. It has remained an important commodity throughout the centuries.

Mustard is made from the seeds of three varieties of mustard plant. Black and white mustards are probably native to the Mediterranean. Indian or brown mustard originated in Africa and spread from there to Asia. Its use can be traced back to the ancient Chinese civilizations at least a thousand years before Christ, and it was used by the ancient Egyptians.

The ancient Greeks and Romans used mustard for flavouring meat. It was probably the Romans who took the seeds to France and then on to Britain.

CULTIVATION AND PRODUCTION

The USSR and Canada are the largest producers of mustard seed, with Canada being the largest exporter. The whole seeds may themselves be used for flavouring, but more usually they are ground and mixed with water or another liquid. France is the largest importer of mustard seed and produces 50,000 tonnes of prepared mustard a year, 90 per cent of which is Dijon mustard.

Some mustards are quite mild; others are extremely hot. In all cases, the mustard seed develops its pungent qualities only after mixing with a cold liquid.

WHITE OR YELLOW MUSTARD
Brassica alba

This is a small, round, hard seed which varies in colour from yellowish brown to white. It originated in central Europe, where it is used as a salad crop. The plant grows quickly,

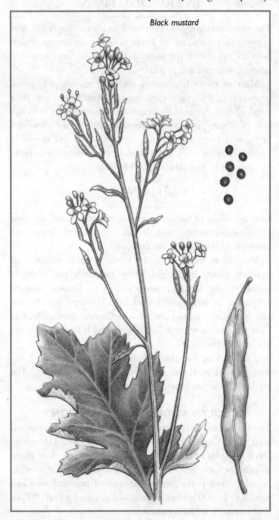

Black mustard

reaching maturity in just a few days. Its light outer skin is removed before sale.

White mustard flour is blander than either black or brown mustard flour as there is only a trace of the volatile oil which contains the heat. Some heat is released when water is added, but with white seed it does not last long.

Analysis of a typical white mustard			
Moisture	8%	Fixed oil	26-28%
Volatile oil	0.2%	Kilo calories	0.4%
Protein	35-40%	Ph 10% solution	6-7
Carbohydrates	21-23%	Storage life	12 months

BLACK MUSTARD

Brassica nigra

This is a small, round, hard seed which varies in colour from dark brown to black. It grows worldwide, but is mainly found in Europe, the USSR, the Middle East, North Africa, India and North America. Black mustard flour has a clean, hot flavour with a slightly bitter taste.

Analysis of a typical black mustard			
Moisture	8%	Fixed oil	40-45%
Volatile oil	0.75%	Kilo calories	0.4%
Protein	30%	Ph 10% solution	6-7
Carbohydrates	16-18%	Storage life	12 months

BROWN OR INDIAN MUSTARD

Brassica juncea

This mustard seed is similar in size to the black variety, but varies in colour from light to dark brown. It is grown in India, southern parts of the USSR, north-eastern Africa and Canada. Brown mustard flour has a similar taste to black mustard flour.

Analysis of a typical brown mustard			
Moisture	8%	Fixed oil	40-45%
Volatile oil	0.8%	Kilo calories	0.4%
Protein	30%	Ph 10% solution	6-7
Carbohydrates	16-18%	Storage life	12 months

COOKING WITH MUSTARD

Mustard helps to bring out the flavour in food, as well as stimulating the palate and aiding digestion. It is most often served as an accompaniment to grills, roasts and cold meats. But it can also be used as a flavouring in sauces, casseroles and soups. Deglaze the pan with cream and mustard after frying veal or pork escalopes, or simply brush mustard over ham and pork joints before roasting. Brush a grainy mustard on mackerel for grilling, or spread a Dijon mustard over herring fillets, roll up and bake with red wine.

Mustard acts as an emulsifier in the preparation of mayonnaises and salad dressings. The whole and ground seeds are also widely used in Indian cooking. Mustard loses some of its pungency when it is cooked. Whole fried mustard seeds, for example, are not very spicy; hot sauces flavoured with mustard can be quite mild.

Mustard can be made at home by mixing mustard flour with water, milk, fruit juice, vinegar, beer, cider or wine. Country-style mustards can be made by crushing mustard seeds and mixing them with herbs, spices and any of the above liquids. Leave the mixture to stand for 15 minutes: this will allow the flavour to develop properly.

Storing mustard

Whole mustard seed and mustard flour can be kept for a year or more in an airtight tin; after this, it starts to lose colour and strength. Ready-made mustard should be stored in a cool place and used within a year.

FRENCH MUSTARD

France produces about half the world's prepared mustard. It is made mainly from brown and some black seeds. Yellow mustard seed may not legally be marketed as mustard in France; instead it is called *condiment*. The main varieties of French mustards are Dijon mustard, Meaux mustard and Bordeaux mustard.

The production of mustard in eastern and southern France can be traced back to early times. By the 13th century, Dijon was recognized as a centre for mustard-making. In the 15th century, laws were introduced to regulate and standardize production, and in 1937 Dijon mustard gained its own *Appellation Contrôllée d'Origine*. Dijon is now considered the mustard capital of the world.

To make French mustard, the mustard seeds are mixed and cleaned, and a dilute liquid is then added. This is usually a blend of vinegar, water and salt, but it could be made up of white wine must, white or red wine or a mixture of vinegar and wine. The liquid and seeds are ground or milled together to produce a paste. In the manufacture of Dijon mustard, which must not contain more than two per cent of ground husks, this paste is put into a centrifuge to spin off the husks. It is then ground again and matured in vats. Dijon mustard has become the generic term for mustard made in this way. In the manufacture of grain mustard, or *moutarde à la methode ancienne,* the husks are not removed.

Mustard is easy to make, but the quality depends on the basic ingredients used. This includes the quality of the mustard seed, the quality and type of vinegar or wine used, the amount of salt added and the quality of any additional herbs or additives. Many of the large firms add colour and preservatives to stabilize the mustard.

Dijon mustard

This is known in France as *moutarde de Dijon* or *moutarde forte.* Dijon mustard is made from a mixture of black and brown seeds blended with vinegar or wine, salt and spices. It is pale yellow and smooth in texture, varying in strength from mild to very hot.

Meaux mustard

This is a grainy mustard made from partly crushed and partly ground black mustard seed, blended with vinegar and spices. Meaux mustard has a speckled appearance and is crunchy in texture; its flavour is medium hot.

Bordeaux mustard

This is also known in France as *moutarde brune.* Bordeaux mustard is made from black mustard seed blended with unfermented wine must. It is dark in colour and fairly mild; it is sometimes flavoured with tarragon.

ENGLISH MUSTARD

Most of the seed used in English mustard is yellow or white mustard. A little brown or black mustard may also be used in the blend. Some English mustard is sold as dry powder, but 83 per cent is sold ready-made.

To make English mustard flour, the seeds are cleaned and dried. The husks are split open in the mill and separated from the kernel by sieving. The kernel is then reduced to a fine powder by rolling and further sieving. The different varieties of mustard seed are powdered separately and then blended according to the type of mustard to be produced; usually English mustard flour is also blended with a small percentage of wheat flour and some spices.

The ingredients for ready-made English mustard include water, mustard flour, sugar, salt, wheat flour, citric acid, and the colourings E171 and E102. Some English versions of ready-made French mustard are made from a mixture of water, spirit vinegar, mustard flour, wheat flour, salt, sugar, modified starch, spices and herbs.

Some wholegrain mustards are also produced in the UK and these are not mixed with flour or any other dry ingredients. Many of them are made by small producers using strictly traditional methods and recipes.

GERMAN MUSTARD

This is usually a smooth blend of black mustard and vinegar. It may be pale yellow or golden, varying from mild to quite hot; it can also be quite sweet. *Weisswurstsenf* is a mild, pale, coarse-grained mustard made to accompany veal sausages.

AMERICAN MUSTARD

This is usually made from white mustard seed blended with sugar, wine or vinegar. It is pale yellow and thinner than most other mustards, with a mild, sweet taste.

OTHER MUSTARDS

Like German mustard, Polish and Swedish mustards tend to be sweet. The Scandinavians also use a lot of Dijon mustard. Oriental mustards are often very hot.

Mustards may be flavoured with a variety of herbs, spices and liquids. Here is a list of some of the flavoured mustards which can be found in good food shops:

Basil mustard	Green pepper mustard	Orange mustard
Beer mustard	Herb mustard	Paprika mustard
Black olive mustard	Honey mustard	Raspberry mustard
Celery mustard	Horseradish mustard	Rosemary mustard
Cider mustard	Lemon mustard	Tarragon mustard
Garlic mustard	Mint mustard	Thyme mustard

GARLIC, HORSERADISH & CAPERS

GARLIC

Allium sativum

Garlic is one of the most important of all flavourings and one which is generally either adored or detested. It is an indispensable ingredient of many Mediterranean dishes. It has also been used for centuries in medicine as a cure-all, and is still taken as garlic oil capsules today. In the First World War, the juice was used extensively on wounds, and in the USSR a compound made from garlic is known as "Russian penicillin".

Garlic is the bulb of a lily-like plant. It is similar in shape to a small onion, but not as smoothly curved. A garlic bulb may consist of anything up to 20 segments, called cloves; usually there are about ten cloves to a bulb. They are separated by tough membranes and enclosed in a brittle parchment-like skin.

Garlic varies in size and colour from big, mild-flavoured, white-skinned varieties to smaller, pink or purple-skinned varieties. The flesh of the clove is usually ivory-coloured, but some, like the French *Rose d'Auvergne,* have a pink skin. The cloves in a bulb should be tightly packed. Loose cloves are a sign of deteriorating or inferior garlic. Garlic is best bought whole, but it can also be bought minced in jars, or dried into granules or powder.

Cultivation

Garlic has been in cultivation for so long that it is impossible to determine exactly where it originated, but Asia is the most likely continent. It is now grown in most temperate areas, particularly around the Mediterranean.

Cooking with garlic

Cloves should be separated from the bulb as required. The clove can be peeled with a knife or crushed first and the peel subsequently picked out. The peeled clove may be sliced, chopped or crushed for use. When crushing garlic with the tip of a knife or fork, it is a good idea to add a little salt in order to catch the juices which might otherwise be lost. This also helps to prevent the pieces slipping about.

Garlic can be extremely strong in flavour and should be used with care in uncooked dishes. A cut clove rubbed once over the surface of the bowl may be sufficient for salads. Cooking reduces the flavour somewhat.

Small amounts will simply help to lift the flavour of a dish, but remain undetected. Large amounts are needed for the Mediterranean classics, and for Indian and Chinese cooking. Whole cloves or bulbs can be roasted or fried to produce a mild, almost sweet-tasting vegetable.

Garlic goes well with most foods. Garlic butters accompany shellfish and grills of fish or meat, while garlic bread is a favourite with buffet meals and barbecues. Pasta dishes often use sauces which are heavy on garlic. An excellent flavouring for pasta can be obtained simply by frying sliced garlic in olive oil. Remove the garlic with a slotted spoon and use the oil to toss the pasta. Many mayonnaises and other cold sauces and dressings also use large amounts of garlic.

Storing garlic

Care should be taken not to damage garlic. Once the cell structure of the bulb is damaged, oxidation quickly spoils the flavour. Keep bulbs in a cool, dry atmosphere, removing and using cloves as required. Fresh garlic will keep for anything from three to six months, depending on the variety and the conditions of storage. Once the bulb starts to develop shoots it becomes rather harsh and coarse. Processed garlic must be kept in airtight containers or it will soon lose its flavour.

HORSERADISH

Armoracia rusticana

Horseradish is a cylindrical white root with a yellowish brown skin. It is sold fresh – whole or grated. In the latter form it is usually preserved in vinegar. Dried, flaked or powdered horseradish is also sold. This retains its pungency for longer than grated horseradish.

Horseradish probably originated in south-eastern Europe, but it now grows in Britain, in the other countries of northern Europe and in the USA. It grows so well that it has become a horticultural pest in some areas.

Cooking with horseradish

Horseradish only becomes pungent when it is broken or bruised. It loses much of its pungency when it is cooked and so it is most often used cold.

When preparing horseradish at home, scrub the root under running water to remove any soil and trim off any fibrous roots. Peel and grate, discarding the central core which is hard and has little or no flavour. Store the grated root in the freezer.

The flavour of horseradish is similar to that of watercress, but hotter and sharper. Its main use is in horseradish sauce. This is made by mixing the grated root with sugar and vinegar; cream or yoghurt may also be added.

In the UK, horseradish sauce is eaten as a classic accompaniment to roast beef. It also complements tongue, sausages and ham. It is good with fish, particularly smoked trout or mackerel. In Scandinavia, eastern Europe and Germany it is used to flavour a variety of soups, stews and sauces, as well as cream cheese. In Japan, finely grated horseradish is mixed into a paste on its own or with mustard and served with *sushi* and *tempura*.

Unusual applications for horseradish include: horseradish butter with grilled fish; horseradish and tomato sauce for shellfish; horseradish and grated apple relish; horseradish and beetroot pickle; and horseradish and yoghurt topping as an accompaniment for jacket potatoes.

CAPERS

Capparis spinosa

Capers are the unopened flower-buds of a straggling spiky bush which is native to the Mediterranean. It is well suited to dry, stony ground and hot summers. The flower-buds are picked by hand from June to August.

Capers are produced in Italy, Spain and North Africa. The smallest flower-buds are the most prized and the most expensive. There are about five different gradings of capers and there is a noticeable difference in taste between each size. Capers may be pickled in either vinegar or salt.

VEGETABLE PASTES AND PUREES

There are many different vegetable pastes and purées available. Some are simply designed as labour-saving ways of buying such flavourings as horseradish, garlic or root ginger. Others are sophisticated products which can be served on their own, spread on canapés, or used as flavourings for stews, casseroles and sauces.

Pastes and purées mostly have a strong, concentrated flavour and one spoonful is usually enough to add extra taste. Try mixing them with cream, yoghurt or soured cream and use to toss pasta. Olive paste and *piccante* paste are particularly good spread over puff or flaky pastry to make interesting canapés. Mix pastes with breadcrumbs and use them as stuffings for rolled roasts, or spread over escalopes and fold up to make veal or beef olives with a difference. Brush lamb joints with sun-dried tomato paste or use artichoke paste to make a cream sauce for chicken.

BLACK OLIVE PASTE

This paste is made all over Europe wherever the olive tree is found. Methods of production vary, but the basic process is the same everywhere. The olives are picked when ripe and stored in a herbed brine for some months. They are then stoned and crushed to a paste. Salt and olive oil are added to preserve the olives and the mixture is bottled. No preservatives are needed if the containers are vacuum-packed. The olive paste will last indefinitely as long as the pots are not opened.

GREEN OLIVE PASTE

This is made in the same way as black olive paste, but the olives are picked when less ripe; that is, when they are still green. Fewer herbs are used.

SUN-DRIED TOMATO PASTE

This is usually made from Mediterranean tomatoes which have been split open and dried in the sun. Various local herbs are added and the mixture is packed in olive oil. When puréed, these tomatoes are called sun-dried tomato paste.

PICCANTE (HOT CHILLI PASTE)

This is a paste for making the famous *Pasta Arrabbiata* sauce. *Arrabbiato* means "angry" and this paste certainly has a hot taste. The ingredients are chillies, olive oil, garlic, coriander and other herbs.

Globe artichoke

ARTICHOKE PASTE

This is a paste made from the hearts of Italian artichokes, which are much smaller than French artichoke hearts. The hearts are chopped up and then mixed with other flavourings – vinegar, salt and herbs. The resulting artichoke paste has a fine, delicate flavour.

PESTO (BASIL SAUCE)

This is a famous sauce from Genoa on the Ligurian coast of Italy. One of the most important aspects of this sauce is the quality of the basil used. Basil is grown in many countries and there are many different varieties. The Ligurian variety is the best for making *Pesto*. The usual ingredients are basil, garlic, *Parmesan* and *Sardo* cheese, salt, pinenuts and oil. (See page 120 for the recipe.)

TAPENADE

This is a French black olive paste comprising crushed black olives, olive oil, salt, capers and a little anchovy. Often the capers and anchovy are left out, but not in the true *Tapenade*.

ANCHOIADE

This is an anchovy and black olive paste made in Provence.

WALNUT SAUCE

This is a pasta sauce comprising olive oil, walnuts, *Parmesan* cheese, pinenuts, herbs and salt.

HERBS AND SPICES

Herbs are plants which have a particularly strong or fragrant taste. They are usually succulent plants which do not develop woody tissues. The leaves and flowers of the plant are most often used as herbs – either fresh or dried.

Spices are the dried parts of aromatic, usually tropical, plants. They are taken from bark, berries, roots or even dried flower-buds. In the kitchen, the terms herbs and spices are often confused. Certain parts of a plant may be referred to as herbs while other parts of the same plant are labelled spices. The leaves of coriander, for example, are classed as herbs and the dried fruit or seeds as spices.

In the past, herbs and spices were considered highly valuable commodities – partly because of the absence of refrigeration as a means of keeping food fresh, and partly because of their scarcity. Some important spices grew only in certain areas, such as the Spice Islands (present-day Indonesia). They were used mainly as preservatives and helped to disguise the "off taste" of old food.

In medieval times, an important spice trade grew up between East and West. For a long time this was controlled by the merchants of the Middle East. Then, in the 15th century, the Portuguese discovered the Spice Islands and began to dominate the spice trade. They were followed by the Dutch, who maintained a stranglehold on the Spice Islands until the islanders rebelled and the Dutch East India Company went bankrupt. Once the Spice Islands monopoly was broken, the seeds of spice-producing plants were taken to other tropical regions and new spice industries grew up.

CULTIVATION AND PRODUCTION

In the past, wild herbs were gathered from the countryside. This is still the practice in some countries. However, in

Europe and the USA, special herb farms have been set up to grow fresh herbs for sale both to retail outlets and to dried herb manufacturers. With the advent of modern packaging and transport, fresh herbs are appearing in more and more supermarkets; they are often available all the year round.

Spices, too, were originally gathered from wild trees and plants. Today spices are farmed on huge plantations in a variety of tropical countries. There is a wide range of spices on sale in most supermarkets. More unusual spices can be found in Arabic, Indian and Chinese stores.

HERBS AND SPICES IN COOKING

Herbs and spices have had various important uses throughout the ages. They have been used in medicine for centuries and some of them still find their way into modern preparations. Some herbs and spices, such as saffron and turmeric, may be used as dyes; others turn up in cosmetics and toiletries of all kinds. However, their most common use everywhere is culinary.

Herbs and spices have a place in almost every kind of cooking. They can be used in salads and starters, soups and stews. They also turn up in desserts, biscuits and cakes. They are even used to flavour and garnish drinks.

At one time, cooks could use only those herbs and spices which grew nearby or which were occasionally brought back from long journeys abroad. Thus different traditions have grown up for their use in classic European cuisine, in Indian curries and in Mexican cooking. Today, these traditional barriers are breaking down and many more herbs and spices are in use outside their indigenous regions.

Some herbs and spices are naturally more pungent than others. Some, like chilli, ginger and paprika are "hot"; if used in too large a quantity these will impart a burning sensation to the mouth. Others, like dill, chervil and basil, are softer and sweeter.

Herbs, particularly, vary in the strength of flavour which they lend to dishes. This flavour comes from the essential oils in the leaves. Chopping herbs helps to release their essential oils and give extra flavour to the food. Herbs such as rosemary, thyme, sage and tarragon, which do not possess very volatile essential oils, have strong flavours; they should be used sparingly. Long cooking brings out their flavour and for this reason they are particularly useful in soups, stews and casseroles. Parsley, basil, chervil and chives, on the other hand, possess very volatile oils and their flavour starts to diminish as soon as they are cut. Cooking can drive out their flavour completely. These herbs are best used raw or should be added towards the end of the cooking time. Chives, in particular, have such a volatile oil that they should always be added after the dish has been removed from the heat.

All herbs are best used fresh, but those with less volatile essential oils do not lose or change their flavour on drying. Indeed, dried herbs have an even stronger flavour than fresh herbs and should be used in smaller quantities. The water content of fresh herbs may be as high as 80 per cent: thus one-quarter to one-third of a teaspoon of dried herbs will be equivalent to one teaspoon of freshly chopped herbs.

Spices may be used whole or ground, but the way they are used will make a difference to the flavour of the finished dish. The way in which they are cooked will also make a difference. Fried ground cumin will taste quite different to toasted ground cumin. This is why the taste of Indian dishes may vary considerably even though they appear to have the same list of spices in the ingredients.

Storing herbs and spices

Herbs are best picked straight from the pot or garden plant. However, if you cannot grow them yourself, store the cut stems in a jar of water inside a polythene bag in the fridge. Chopped herbs can be stored in cubes of ice in the freezer.

Dried herbs and spices should be stored in well-stoppered jars away from light. Always buy from a stockist with a rapid turnover of spices and do not store at home for too long or they will lose their flavour.

MIXED HERBS AND SPICES

Herbs and spices may be used singly or in combination. There is no reason why you should not create your own herb combinations, but remember that some herbs combine much better than others. Parsley, chives and chervil will mix with most things but herbs like rosemary, dill, marjoram, mint, oregano and thyme, which have a very strong flavour, need more care. They mix well with the milder herbs but should not be used too heavily. Tarragon and basil are also strongly flavoured but they complement rather than compete with other herbs such as rosemary and thyme. Experiment to get the best results.

In the meantime, here is a short selection of tried and trusted herb combinations:

■ chives, dill and mint in equal proportions
■ chervil and tarragon in equal proportions
■ ⅔ parsley to ⅓ mint

■ ½ parsley to ⅙ each of rosemary, thyme and fennel
■ basil, tarragon and parsley in equal quantities
■ parsley and chives in equal quantities, together with a little fresh coriander

Over the years, some classic combinations have been developed. The four most common mixtures are *bouquet garni, fines herbes,* mixed herbs and *garam masala.*

BOUQUET GARNI

This French mixture is usually tied together and wrapped into a small bundle with slices of celery or some leek leaves. The bundle should always contain a bayleaf, a sprig of thyme and two or three sprigs of parsley. Sometimes other herbs like chervil, savory or tarragon are added.

FINES HERBES

This term is sometimes used to mean chopped parsley alone. However, in classic French cuisine it should include a mixture of parsley, chervil, tarragon and chives.

MIXED HERBS

This is really an Anglicized version of *fines herbes* and may contain any mixture of herbs. A common mixture is marjoram, thyme, rosemary and parsley.

GARAM MASALA

This is the Indian name for a mixture of spices. There is no word for "curry" in the Indian language and curry powder does not exist as a specific mixture of spices. There are many, many different spice mixes. One mixture which is used to add spiciness to an Indian dish towards the end of the cooking time consists of two teaspoons of ground cardomom and one teaspoon each of ground cinnamon, cloves, black pepper and cumin.

MAIN TYPES OF HERBS

The main types of herbs used singly in cooking are basil, bay leaves, chervil, chives, coriander, dill, marjoram, mint, oregano, parsley, rosemary, sage, tarragon and thyme.

BASIL

Ocimum basilicum

Basil is a low-growing annual. It has sizeable green silky leaves, which are stripped from the stem and used fresh in cooking. The flavour is quite strong and aromatic. However, very large-leafed varieties do not have such a good flavour.

Basil

Basil has a longer culinary history than most other herbs. It probably came from India to Europe via the Middle East. It was known to the ancient Egyptians, who passed their knowledge on to the Arabs, Greeks and Romans.

Uses: raw in salads, particularly with tomatoes. Use with garlic for best effect when cooking in stews and sauces. It also goes well with mushrooms and in combinations of herbs such as rosemary and sage.

Classic dishes: *Pesto* sauce for pasta, *Pistou* sauce for soup

BAY LEAVES
Laurus nobilis

The sweet bay tree is a small shrub with tough, green, oval leaves which are stripped from the branches for use in cooking. The leaves, which may be used fresh or dried, have a spicy flavour. Bay is native to the Mediterranean and was known in ancient Greece.

Uses: in *bouquet garni*, soups, stocks, marinades and stews

CHERVIL
Anthriscus cerifolium

Chervil is a small, almost feathery herb with a light, sweet flavour of aniseed. Use it fresh in quite large quantities.

Uses: in salads and garnishes and in herb mixtures of all kinds. The French tend to use chervil in place of parsley.

Classic dishes: German chervil soup, served during Lent

CHIVES
Allium schoenoprasum

The chive is a slim green member of the onion family. The essential oil of chives is extremely volatile so chives should only be used fresh as an addition to raw food, or as an addition to cooked food once the cooking is complete.

Uses: to flavour cream cheese and potato dishes, salads and cooked vegetables

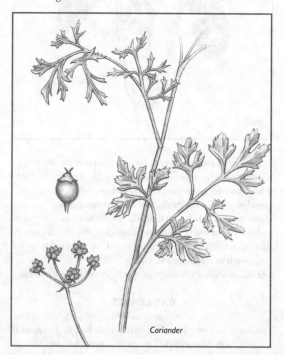

Coriander

CORIANDER

Coriandrum sativum

The attractive leaves of this small plant resemble continental parsley, but the difference may be detected by rubbing the herb between the fingers, which releases a distinctive smell. The seeds are also dried for use as spices (see page 79). Use the leaves fresh.

Uses: chopped in salads or as a garnish for oriental soups and main course dishes. Use with care in cooked foods as the flavour can be very bitter. It goes well with curries and with Thai and Vietnamese cooking.

DILL

Peucedanum graveolens or *Anethum graveolens*

This small, feathery plant has a unique but mild flavour. It is found growing wild in southern Europe. It may be used fresh or dried.

Uses: added at the last minute to fish dishes, soups and potato dishes, or used with cucumber or salads. Dill seed is also used to make pickles and dill vinegar.

Classic dishes: dill pickles

MARJORAM

Origanum majorana

Sweet marjoram is an annual. The leaves may be used fresh or dried. It was used extensively by the ancient Greeks, who gave it its name.

Uses: to flavour meats and stuffings and in mixed herbs with thyme

MINT

Mentha viridis or *spicata* (spearmint)
Mentha rotundifolia (applemint)

There are many different varieties of mint. It is particularly popular in English gardens where spearmint or applemint predominate. Mint is believed to have originated in the Far East, coming to Europe via Africa. Use fresh.

Uses: in sauces, salads and soups, and for flavouring new potatoes and peas

Classic dishes: mint sauce or jelly

OREGANO

Origanum vulgare

Oregano is a variety of wild marjoram, but has a much stronger flavour than marjoram. It can be used both fresh and dried in cooking.

Uses: as a strong flavouring for soups, stews and casseroles. It is used extensively in Italian cooking in pizzas and tomato-based sauces.

PARSLEY

Petroselinum crispum (curly parsley)

There are a number of different varieties of this biennial plant. Curly varieties, which are popular in the UK, have deeply divided leaves, each division curling over to give the plant a crinkly, decorative appearance. Flat-leafed varieties are popular on the Continent, where they are used mainly for garnish. Both types should be used fresh.

Uses: in *bouquet garni* and most other herb mixtures as well as in sauces, vegetable dishes, soups and stews

Classic dishes: in parsley sauce for fish or butter beans, and in *jambon persillade*

ROSEMARY

Rosmarinus officinalis

This aromatic shrub has deeply divided spiky leaves. It may be used fresh or dried; either way, use it sparingly.

Uses: as a standard addition to all kinds of meat and fish dishes in Italy. It also goes well with fried potatoes, *risotto* and cooked vegetables. It can be used very successfully in sweet dishes, such as jellies and fruit salads, and in cider and claret cups.

SAGE

Salvia officinalis

There are over 500 species of *Salvia*. The most common, *officinalis*, is a small shrub with silvery green leaves. These are stripped from the stem and may be used fresh or dried. Red sage and narrow-leafed sage are the best-known of the other varieties. The herb was known in ancient Greek and Roman times when it was used as a remedy for snakebites.

Uses: used frequently with fatty dishes such as roast goose, duck and pork; it is also served with eel. It may be added to salads, kebabs and pickles.

Classic dishes: sage and onion stuffing and calves' liver with sage

TARRAGON

Artesemisia dranunculus

The variety of this herb which is mainly chosen for cooking is French tarragon, also known as true tarragon. It is a small plant with long tapering leaves, which may be used fresh or

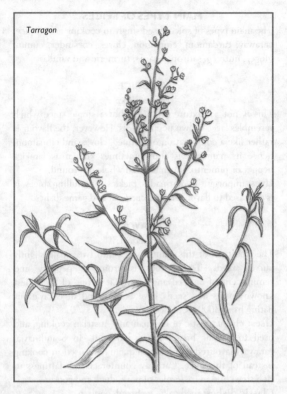

Tarragon

dried. Russian tarragon looks similar to French, but it has very little taste.

Uses: used widely in French cooking, often with chervil, and in fresh salads and wine vinegar. It sometimes forms a part of classic herb mixtures and is used to flavour sauces, mayonnaise, butters and grills.

Classic dishes: Bearnaise sauce, chicken with tarragon

THYME

Thymus vulgaris

There are over 100 species of thyme, all developed from wild thyme, but garden thyme is the variety most frequently grown for culinary use. It has been used in European cooking since Greek and Roman times.

Uses: as an almost universal flavouring. It is used with all meats, fish and vegetables and is an essential part of a *bouquet garni*.

Classic dishes: thyme and onion stuffing

MAIN TYPES OF SPICES

The main types of spices used singly in cooking are allspice, caraway, cardamom, cinnamon, cloves, coriander, cumin, ginger, nutmeg, saffron, sesame, turmeric and vanilla.

ALLSPICE
Pimenta dioica

This is not a mixture of spices, but a single spice which resembles large brown peppercorns. However, the flavour is rather like a combination of nutmeg, cloves and cinnamon, hence its name. It is also sometimes known as Jamaica pepper or pimento. It can be used whole or ground.

Uses: important in marinades, pickles and mulling spices. It is also used to flavour soups, *sauerkraut* and game dishes.

CARAWAY
Carum carvi

The ripe fruit of this plant divides into two small, slightly curved seeds. The flavour is aromatic, peppery and reminiscent of aniseed and fennel. It is one of the oldest known spices and seeds have been found in excavations dating from 3000 BC. Use whole.

Uses: characteristic of German and Austrian cooking, and used to flavour bread, cakes and fruit. In Scandinavia, caraway-flavoured spirits and liqueurs are used in cooking instead of the spice. Caraway counteracts the fattiness in rich stews and in casseroles of pork, duck and goose.

Classic dishes: seed cake, ryebread, goulash

CARDAMOM
Elettaria cardamomum

The small black seeds of the cardamom are contained in round pods. It is best to buy the whole pods and to remove the seeds as required, because ground cardamom quickly loses its flavour.

Uses: in curries, in Chinese, Indian and Middle Eastern desserts and in mulled wine. It is also used to flavour Greek and Turkish coffee.

Classic dishes: *pilau* rice

CINNAMON
Cinnamomum zeylanicum

Cinnamon is the dried, rolled inner bark from the shoots of a small tropical tree. The spice is sold ground or in the form of small cylinders of bark or quills. It is known to have been used by the ancient Chinese and Egyptians.

Uses: used extensively in both Eastern and Western cooking. It has a variety of applications in baking, milk puddings, chocolate dishes, stuffings, stews, rice, curries and mulled wine.

Classic dishes: cinnamon toast

CLOVES
Eugenia caryophyllus

Cloves are the immature dried flower-buds of a tropical plant, native to the Moluccas or Spice Islands. They are best used whole; ground cloves soon lose their flavour. Fresh cloves should be used sparingly as they are very pungent.

Uses: important in Eastern and Western cooking in both sweet and savoury dishes. In the West, cloves are commonly used to stud baked ham and to flavour baked apple dishes. They may also be used in casseroles, gravies and smoked meats. In the East, they are used in curries.

CORIANDER
Coriandrum sativum

The dried seeds of the coriander plant are used as a spice in Eastern and Middle Eastern cooking. They may be used whole or ground. The flavour is warm and aromatic with a citrus undertone, reminiscent of orange peel.

Uses: in curries, soups and stews. In the West, it is used in black pudding and in *mortadella* sausage. It is also widely used in Arabic cooking.

CUMIN
Cuminum cyminum

Cumin is the small split seed of an umbelliferous plant. The seeds may be used whole or ground. If used whole, the seeds should be lightly toasted first to bring out the flavour. Cumin has a long history of culinary usage dating back to ancient Egypt.

Uses: used mainly where highly spiced food is preferred. It is an ingredient in Indian curries, Mexican *encheladas*, Middle Eastern lamb dishes and Dutch *Gouda* cheese.

Classic dishes: *chile con carne*

GINGER
Zingiber officinale

Ginger is available in a variety of forms. Fresh or "green" ginger is the bulbous root of the ginger plant; it should be peeled and chopped, or grated for use. Dried ginger is available whole or ground; it has a hot peppery taste quite different to the fresh root. Young "stem" ginger may be preserved in syrup or crystallized; both these preparations tend to be quite hot. Fresh ginger is also sold ground and mixed with lemon juice.

Uses: mainly used in the West in its ground form to flavour cakes, biscuits and preserves. Fresh ginger is used in a large number of savoury dishes in India, Indonesia, China and Japan. The ground root may be used in *garam masala*.

Classic dishes: brandy snaps and gingerbread

NUTMEG
Myristica fragrans

This is the fruit of a large tree native to the Moluccas or Spice Islands. The nut is usually sold separate from its shell and enclosing aril. The aril dries to a yellowish brown colour and is sold as mace. Nutmeg can be used grated or ground in cooking.

Uses: used widely in Europe to flavour pies, puddings and custards as well as bread, egg and vegetable dishes. It is also used in the Caribbean and in India to flavour sweet desserts.

Classic dishes: custard tarts

SAFFRON
Crocus sativus

Saffron comes from the inner part of the flower of a small crocus. It consists of the delicate, thread-like stigmas. The best saffron is bright orange and does not have any white or yellow strands mixed in with it. Saffron is a very expensive spice because it takes 70,000 flowers to produce 450 grams of saffron. However, it does not take much saffron to flavour quite large quantities of food. It is available whole or roasted and ground. Whole saffron should first be steeped in a small amount of hot water and the strained liquid then added to the dish.

Uses: most commonly used to colour rice. It is also used in Indian festive cooking and in some Middle Eastern dishes.

Classic dishes: saffron cake, *paella* and *bouillabaisse*

SESAME
Sesamum indicum

Sesame seeds are sold dried or are made into a paste called *tahini*, which resembles peanut butter. The flavour of the dried seeds is intensified by toasting.

Uses: sprinkled over cakes, biscuits and bread, and in Middle Eastern, Indian and Far Eastern dishes.

Classic dishes: sesame buns, *hummus, halva*

SPICE CHART: ORIGINS AND PRODUCTION

Spice	Regions of origin	Modern producing regions
Allspice	West Indies, South & Central America	Plantations in the West Indies, particularly Jamaica; collected wild in South and Central America
Caraway	Asia Minor	All over Europe, particularly in Holland and Germany, as well as in the Soviet Union, Turkey, India and North Africa
Cardamom	India	Sri Lanka, India, Guatemala, South-east Asia and Tanzania
Cinnamon	Sri Lanka	India, Brazil, Indonesia, the West Indies and the islands of the Indian Ocean
Cloves	Molucca Islands	Brazil, Indonesia, the West Indies, Mauritius, India, Sri Lanka, Tanzania and Madagascar
Coriander	Middle East and southern Europe	India, the Soviet Union, South America, North Africa (particularly Morocco), and Holland
Cumin	Levant and Upper Egypt	India, North Africa, China and the Americas
Ginger	South-east Asia	India, Pakistan, Jamaica, Central and South America, China, Japan, Africa and Australia
Nutmeg	Molucca Islands	Indonesia, West Indies, Malaysia and Sri Lanka
Saffron	Greece or Asia Minor	Mediterranean Europe, particularly Spain, as well as India, Turkey, Iran and China
Sesame	India	India, China, Asia, the Americas and Africa
Turmeric	South-east Asia	India, Sri Lanka, Indonesia, China, Taiwan, Africa, Australia and the West Indies
Vanilla	Mexico	Mexico, the Seychelles, Madagascar and Indonesia

TURMERIC
Curcuma domestica

This is the rhizome of a ginger-like plant. It may be used whole, ground or fresh.

Uses: often used as a colouring ingredient in place of saffron, though the flavour is quite different. It is common in curries and in Indian desserts.

Classic dishes: kedgeree

VANILLA
Vanilla fragrans

This flavouring comes from the seed or bean of the vanilla plant. It may be sold as a whole bean or as a liquid essence. True vanilla is highly fragrant, but the much cheaper artificial flavouring is harsh and has a nasty aftertaste; it is best avoided.

Uses: as a flavouring for ice cream, milk puddings, sweet egg dishes and sweetmeats such as fudge and toffee

PEPPER

The name "pepper" is applied to the pungent, dried fruit or seeds of a variety of plants. The main culinary varieties are true pepper (table pepper), cayenne pepper, chilli pepper, paprika pepper and pink pepper.

CULTIVATION AND PRODUCTION

True pepper is native to south-eastern India and Cambodia, but it is now cultivated in the West Indies, Indonesia and other tropical Asian countries.

Chilli peppers are native to South America and are now grown extensively throughout the tropics and sub-tropics. The main areas of production are India (which is the world's largest producer), Mexico, the USA, the West Indies, Indonesia and West Africa.

COOKING WITH PEPPER

As a condiment, black or white pepper is present on almost every Western table and it is used in virtually all savoury cooking. Whole peppercorns are used in stocks and pickling mixtures; they can also be lightly crushed and used as a coating for grilled or fried meats. Coarsely ground pepper may be used to coat soft cheeses and salami-style sausages.

Black and white pepper is best bought whole and ground at home, because ready-powdered pepper quickly loses its flavour. Peppercorns can easily be ground in a peppermill. If cracked or crushed pepper is required, simply place the whole peppercorns in a polythene bag and crush them with a rolling pin. Green peppercorns which have been dried can be re-constituted by soaking in a little cold water.

Paprika, cayenne and chilli peppers are also used as condiments in countries where spicy food is particularly popular. Paprika is a classic ingredient in Hungarian goulash, Spanish spiced sausages and *Tandoori* chicken. Cayenne is hotter and more pungent than the average paprika pepper and a small amount adds piquancy to stews, casseroles and sauces. It is good with devilled dishes and also with potted shrimps and grilled meats.

Some chilli peppers are quite literally so hot that they can burn. Those sold in Europe do not need to be handled with protective gloves, but take care not to rub the eyes or sensitive skin with the hands while preparing chillies. Always wash your hands when you have finished the job.

Much of the heat of chilli peppers lies in the seeds, so remove these from both fresh and dried chillies if you do not want your cooking to be too hot. If you overseason with chilli, a little sugar may help to alleviate the hotness.

Chilli is an essential element of Mexican and Caribbean food. It is also used extensively in South America and in West Africa. Sauces which rely heavily on chilli include *harissa* sauce from Tunisia, *hoisin* sauce from the Szechwan region of China and Tabasco sauce from the USA.

Storing pepper

Store whole black and white peppers in a dry place. Ground pepper, chilli powder, cayenne pepper and paprika pepper should all be stored in airtight jars away from light. Do not keep them for too long or the flavour will decline.

TRUE PEPPER OR TABLE PEPPER

True pepper, the so-called "King of Spices", comes from several species of a vinous plant which produce small fruit or peppercorns.

Black and white pepper: *Piper nigrum*

Black pepper is the dried unripe fruit of the plant. The peppercorns are round and wrinkled. White pepper comes from fruit which is picked when almost ripe; the dark outer skin is removed by soaking in water. The peppercorns are slightly smaller than the black ones. Both types of pepper consist of a grey, horny seed with a tiny cavity.

Mignonette or shot pepper

This is a rough-ground mixture of black and white corns widely used in France. It may also be sold as a powder.

Green pepper

This consists of unripe fresh corns. They are usually bottled or canned in brine and they may also be freeze-dried.

Long pepper: *Piper longum*

This consists of a fused mass of minute fruits in the form of a small conical spike. It is not often used in the West.

CAYENNE PEPPER

Capsicum frutescens

This is a finely-ground pepper prepared from the seeds and pods of various types of chilli peppers. It is made from ripe fruit and is red or reddish brown in colour. Some cayenne peppers retain the seeds of the fruit and are hotter than those which exclude them.

CHILLI PEPPER

Capsicum frutescens

Chilli is the common name given to a wide range of different varieties of *Capsicums*. Chillies vary tremendously in size, shape and colour, but they are nearly always associated with hotness and pungency.

Chillies can be bought whole – either unripe, when they are green, or ripe, when they may be red, yellow, brown, purple or black. They may be dried, in which case their colour is most likely to be dark red, brown or black. Flaked, ground or powdered chilli peppers can also be found on sale in most countries.

Chilli powder or red pepper

This is ground powder made from all kinds of chillies. It may be mild to hot, depending on the chillies used. In the United States, oregano and cumin or garlic are sometimes added to the chilli mix.

Chilli seasoning

This is chilli powder mixed with salt and spices, such as cumin or garlic. Again, its taste may vary from mild to hot.

PAPRIKA PEPPER

Capsicum annum

This is a fine powder ground from a number of different varieties of *Capsicums*. The peppers which are used to make paprika are larger and milder than chilli peppers though some paprika pepper can be quite hot. The powder varies in colour from bright red to rusty brown. Several grades of flavour are manufactured, but the choice is limited outside Hungary and Spain. Mild paprika is sweet, adding as much colour as flavour to cooking.

PINK PEPPER

Schirius terebinthifolius

This is not a vinous pepper, but comes from the almost-ripe berries of a South American tree. It is available bottled in vinegar or as dried berries. It is used more as a gourmet curiosity than as a flavouring. However, there have been reports of ill-effects after eating pink peppercorns; it is therefore sensible to limit the number used in a dish or sauce to about a dozen and not to eat them too often.

SALT

Salt is sodium chloride. It is produced all over the world, as rock salt by mining or as sea salt by evaporation. The main culinary varieties are rock salt (halite) and sea salt.

COOKING WITH SALT

Salt is used commercially for curing hides, freezing ice-cream and unfreezing road surfaces. It is also used in the manufacture of caustic soda and laboratory chemicals. Throughout the ages, however, its most important use has been culinary.

The use of salt is universal in savoury dishes; even in sweet baking a small amount is often used to bring out the flavours. Less sea salt is required in cooking than rock salt, because sea salt is more powerful.

Salt has a toughening action, which is why vegetables are often brined before pickling; this process helps to give them a crisp texture. The same toughening action is an important consideration when using salt in grilling, barbecuing and microwave cooking. Always add the salt at the end of the cooking time for these processes, never before.

Salt can be used to draw out the bitter juices in vegetables such as courgettes, cucumbers and aubergines. The process of salting also seems to stop the vegetables absorbing too much fat on subsequent frying.

Storing salt

Salt is inorganic and will keep indefinitely. It does not require airtight storage. However, it will absorb water from the atmosphere and soon becomes damp in humidity. A few grains of rice will help to keep it dry. Do not keep salt in silver salt cellars, because the chlorine in the salt will attack the silver, causing a green discolouration.

Salt and nutrition

Salt is essential to life. It regulates the osmotic tension in the tissues and the blood. Salt deficiency causes severe illness and, if taken far enough, will result in death. On the other hand, too much salt can cause kidney failure. Some experts also believe that excessive salt intake may be associated with high blood pressure. They have suggested that Western diets provide far more salt than is required by the body and that everyone should cut back their intake. However, not all sections of the population are adversely affected by high levels of salt consumption and it is currently impossible to identify those who are most at risk.

ROCK SALT OR HALITE

Halite is the scientific name for rock salt, which occurs in layers from the evaporation of land-locked seas of past geological ages. It is either mechanically or hydraulically mined from huge underground mines.

Rock salt varies in colour and is hard and crystalline. It comes in large lumps which need to be ground down using a pestle and mortar or a special mill. Occasionally it is available as untreated separated crystals. In the USA "rock salt" refers to "freezing salt" which is inedible.

Untreated rock salt is said to have the best flavour of all salts. It is produced all over the world, but some Eastern rock salt has an unpleasant sulphurous smell.

Cooking or kitchen salt

Cooking salt used to come in block form and was simply refined rock salt with no additives. Today it is usually a fairly coarse, free-running, container-packaged rock salt, with added magnesium carbonate.

Table salt

This is usually finely-ground refined rock salt which has been mixed with magnesium carbonate or a similar chemical to provide easy flow for use at table.

Pickling salt

This is refined rock salt for pickling. It has none of the additives used in cooking salt or table salt, which are unsuitable as the chemicals in them cause discolouration and result in slimy pickles.

Black or grey salt

Black salt is unrefined rock salt from Asia. It is available in crystallized lumps which may be dark blue or red because of various trace elements. Grey salt is the same as black salt, but of a grey appearance because of the presence of other trace elements.

Spiced or seasoned salt

This is rock salt with flavouring added. Common additives are celery, garlic or onion.

Pretzel salt

This is a Mexican rock salt popular in the USA. The crystals fuse during baking, but retain a shiny crystalline appearance.

Iodized salt

This is rock salt with added iodine, as the name suggests.

SEA SALT

This is salt which is obtained by the direct evaporation of sea water or the factory-finishing of saline concentrations from sea water pans. Sea salt sometimes contains traces of other salts and elements, but any iodine present is lost during storage.

Sea salt is made up of large pure crystals. It lacks the bitter aftertaste of table salt and also has a more powerful flavour. It can be used at table in a salt mill.

Magnesium carbonate is added to commercially-ground sea salt in order to improve its flow and to prevent the absorption of moisture.

Bay salt or gros sel

Bay salt or *gros sel* is another name for sea salt. It may have originated from the Bay of Biscay.

Maldon salt

This is considered to be the finest English sea salt. It comes from Maldon in Essex. The crystals are soft enough to be sprinkled directly onto food.

Sel gris

This is a coarse, grey sea salt which is commonly used in French kitchens.

RECIPES

The recipes in this section are divided into five main groups: oil and vinegar dressings, mayonnaise and egg-based dressings, marinades, pickles and some general ideas for using flavourings.

All of the recipes are designed for four people, unless otherwise stated. Metric conversions of imperial measurements are not exact, so follow one or other set of measurements for each recipe. In most instances where "salt and pepper" are mentioned, we would recommend the use of freshly-ground black pepper and ground sea salt. Use ready-made mustard unless dry mustard is specified.

OIL AND VINEGAR DRESSINGS

These simple dressings are probably the oldest kind. In ancient oil-producing areas oil was predominant in dressings, but vinegar became the main ingredient in countries – like England – where oil was more difficult to obtain.

Today the recipe for a simple oil and vinegar dressing, also known as a "French dressing" or a "vinaigrette", is as variable as the people who make it. There is no right or wrong way of making such a dressing. What matters is the quality of the ingredients used. It is not surprising that many people need to add a pinch of sugar to their dressing when you taste, on its own, the vinegar they have chosen.

In English-speaking countries, an oil and vinegar dressing is often known as a French dressing, though it is doubtful whether an Italian or Spaniard would accept this attribution. The French gastronomic dictionary *Larousse* describes a vinaigrette as a mixture of oil and vinegar seasoned with salt and pepper, sometimes with the addition of chopped herbs. This definition provides a basic theme around which inspired chefs and home cooks have created variations.

A good olive oil is the base oil most often chosen for the dressing, whether it be a mild blend, or a stronger-flavoured virgin or extra virgin oil. There is, however, no reason why other oils should not be used instead: well-flavoured oils, such as sesame oil or many of the nut oils, can transform a simple salad dish into a feast.

The same kind of quality considerations apply to the vinegar you use in dressings, whether it be a straightforward red or white wine vinegar, cider vinegar or some kind of flavoured vinegar. In France, no one would dream of using anything but red wine vinegar for salads, but in the UK it is more likely to be white.

Additional flavourings are many and varied. The French tend to favour mustard and herbs, while the Spanish use garlic, gherkins and capers. Other ingredients may include cream, blue cheese, hard-boiled eggs, sweet peppers, soy sauce, fruit juices, peanuts and spices.

VINAIGRETTE

The proportions given in *Larousse* are as follows:

3 tablespoons OLIVE OIL
I scant tablespoon WINE VINEGAR
SALT AND PEPPER

Place all the ingredients together in a container and beat with a fork to create a temporary emulsion.

Variations

■ We would recommend increasing the amount of oil to 4 or even 5 tablespoons.

■ An easy way of mixing vinaigrette is to put the ingredients in a small bottle or jam jar. Screw down the lid and shake well.

■ Vinaigrette keeps well, so you may wish to make more than you immediately require and store it in a bottle or jam jar at room temperature.

NUT OIL VINAIGRETTE

Walnut or hazelnut oil can be used in place of olive oil in salad dressings. However, they both have pronounced flavours. If you are looking for something less strong, try mixing them with sunflower or ground-nut oils, which are less distinctive. You may need to experiment to find exactly the right proportions.

Pineseed, pistachio and roasted sesame oils are also strong and should be used sparingly, but they can taste good in vinaigrette. If you make a salad using pinenuts, pistachios or sesame seeds as part of the salad, these oils will help to heighten the flavour.

HOT WALNUT OIL DRESSING

This dressing suits any kind of hot salad. Make the dressing in the pan in which the hot food – scallops, bacon, slices of game bird or chicken livers – has been fried.

I tablespoon **SUNFLOWER OR GROUND-NUT OIL**
4 tablespoons **SHALLOTS OR MILD RED ONIONS, FINELY CHOPPED**
4 tablespoons **WALNUT OIL**
3 tablespoons **RED WINE**
2 tablespoons **RED WINE VINEGAR**
SALT AND PEPPER

Heat the sunflower or ground-nut oil in the frying pan and gently fry the shallots or onions until they are soft. Add the wine, vinegar and seasoning and bring to the boil. Reduce by about half. Gradually whisk in the walnut oil over a low heat. Use hot.

WALNUT AND RASPBERRY VINAIGRETTE

This well-flavoured vinaigrette can be used with meat or game salads as well as with strongly-flavoured leaves like roquette, watercress and sorrel.

3 tablespoons **RASPBERRY VINEGAR**
7 tablespoons **WALNUT OIL**
SALT AND PEPPER

Mix all the ingredients in a bottle or jar and shake well.
Variation
■ Add one teaspoon shallots, finely chopped.

BASIL AND WALNUT VINAIGRETTE

This American-inspired dressing is good on blanched and sliced courgettes, sliced tomatoes or blanched green beans.

I tablespoon **DIJON MUSTARD**
50ml/2fl oz/¼ cup **RED WINE VINEGAR**
I handful **BASIL LEAVES, WELL CHOPPED**
SALT AND PEPPER
200ml/8fl oz/I cup **OLIVE OIL**
50g/2oz/½ cup **WALNUTS, FINELY CHOPPED**

Beat the mustard, vinegar, basil leaves and seasoning together with a fork. Gradually add the oil, beating all the time, and then beat in the nuts.

Variation

■ If this dressing is made in a food processor or blender the result is much thicker, but take care not to over-process. The nuts should be finely chopped, but they should be discernible in the dressing.

WALNUT AND TARRAGON VINAIGRETTE

2 tablespoons RASPBERRY VINEGAR
I teaspoon SHALLOTS OR SPRING ONIONS, FRESHLY CHOPPED
I teaspoon LEMON JUICE
I teaspoon TARRAGON, FRESHLY CHOPPED
SALT AND PEPPER
7 tablespoons WALNUT OIL

Mix all the ingredients except the oil in a container and gradually beat in the oil to form an emulsion. Use at once.

HAZELNUT AND SHERRY VINEGAR DRESSING

This strongly-flavoured dressing is excellent in meat salads. Reduce the quantity of vinegar for salad leaves alone.

4 tablespoons HAZELNUT OIL
2 tablespoons SHERRY VINEGAR
SALT AND PEPPER

Place all the ingredients in a container and beat well to form an emulsion. Use at once.

RASPBERRY VINAIGRETTE

100ml/4fl oz/½ cup OLIVE OIL
75ml/3fl oz/⅓ cup RASPBERRY VINEGAR
I tablespoon RASPBERRY PUREE
SALT AND PEPPER
I tablespoon FROMAGE FRAIS OR QUARK (OPTIONAL)

Beat together the oil, vinegar and raspberry purée. Season to taste. Fold in the *fromage frais* or quark at the end.

Notes

■ The Americans often like to add fruit to their dressings.

■ In this and the following recipe, a British cook may prefer to reduce the proportions of vinegar.

BLUEBERRY VINAIGRETTE

100ml/4fl oz/½ cup **OLIVE OIL**
75ml/3fl oz/⅓ cup **BLUEBERRY OR WHITE WINE VINEGAR**
SALT AND PEPPER
I pinch **CINNAMON**
50g/2oz/½ cup **FRESH BLUEBERRIES**

Beat together the oil and vinegar with the seasoning and cinnamon. Stir in the blueberries just before serving.

MUSTARD VINAIGRETTE

Any kind of mustard can be used in dressings. However, if you choose mustard powder rather than mustard paste, cut the quantity by two-thirds.

4 tablespoons **OLIVE OIL**
I tablespoon **VINEGAR**
I tablespoon **MUSTARD OF YOUR CHOICE**
SALT AND PEPPER

Mix all the ingredients together in a container and beat with a fork to form an emulsion. Use at once.

Variation

■ Add 2 tablespoons tomato juice.

SWEET MUSTARD SAUCE
FOR GRAVLAX

This recipe comes from Sweden. It can be made without the sugar if preferred.

3 tablespoons **MILD MUSTARD**
I tablespoon **CASTOR SUGAR**
I tablespoon **WHITE WINE VINEGAR**
75ml/3fl oz/⅓ cup **CORN OIL**
4 tablespoons **DILL, CHOPPED**
SALT AND PEPPER

Beat the mustard, sugar and wine vinegar in a container. Gradually add the oil in a thin, steady trickle, beating all the time. Stir in the dill and season to taste.

HERB VINAIGRETTE

Any herbs can be used in this dressing, either singly or mixed. But only use fresh herbs, or herbs which keep their flavour well when dried, like thyme, oregano and dill.

3 tablespoons OLIVE OIL
I tablespoon WHITE WINE VINEGAR
I tablespoon HERBS, CHOPPED
SALT AND PEPPER

Place the oil and vinegar in a container and beat together. Add the herbs and seasoning and beat again. Use at once.

VINAIGRETTE MARSEILLAISE

Southern France is known for its generous use of garlic, but this recipe would be appreciated equally well in Spain or southern Italy.

3 tablespoons OLIVE OIL
I scant tablespoon RED WINE VINEGAR
I clove GARLIC, CRUSHED
SALT AND PEPPER

Place all the ingredients together in a container and beat with a fork to form an emulsion. Use at once.

AVOCADO DRESSING

Avocados are very rich in texture and in flavour. This dressing uses a little more vinegar than usual, as well as the sharp flavour of an onion to provide a contrast of flavour and texture.

6 tablespoons OLIVE OIL
3 tablespoons WHITE WINE OR CIDER VINEGAR
SALT AND PEPPER
3 tablespoons SPRING ONIONS OR SHALLOTS, FINELY CHOPPED

Place the oil and vinegar in a container with the seasoning and beat well. Add the chopped onion, beat again and spoon into the avocado halves.

Variation

■ Dill goes well with avocado and could be added, finely chopped, at the same stage as the onion.

Honey Vinaigrette

This is a light, sweet dressing. Remember that the flavour of the honey will affect the result; strong clover honey, for example, may not go well with the other salad ingredients.

4 tablespoons OLIVE OIL
1 tablespoon VINEGAR
1 tablespoon MUSTARD OF YOUR CHOICE
2 teaspoons CLEAR HONEY

Mix all the ingredients in a container and beat with a fork to form an emulsion. Use at once.

English Dressing

This is a fairly universal dressing which is found in many parts of the world, not just in the UK.

100ml/4fl oz/½ cup SALAD OIL OF YOUR CHOICE
3 tablespoons WINE VINEGAR
½ teaspoon DIJON MUSTARD
SALT AND BLACK PEPPER
½ clove GARLIC, CRUSHED

Place all the ingredients together in a container and beat with a fork to form an emulsion. Use at once.

Spanish Spicy Dressing

This popular Spanish recipe is used on a variety of cold vegetables for *Tapas*. It is particularly good with carrots.

2 large cloves GARLIC, CRUSHED
1 teaspoon OREGANO, CHOPPED
½ teaspoon GROUND CUMIN
½ teaspoon GROUND CORIANDER
1 pinch DRIED HOT RED PEPPER FLAKES
SALT AND PEPPER
50ml/2fl oz/¼ cup OLIVE OIL
3 teaspoons SHERRY VINEGAR

Grind the garlic, oregano, spices and seasoning using a pestle and mortar. Transfer to a bowl and gradually add the vinegar to form a paste. Next add the olive oil in a thin, steady stream, beating all the time, to form an emulsion. Use at once.

Makes sufficient for 450g/1lb vegetables.

LEBANESE SALAD DRESSING

This dressing is usually served on a mixed salad of green leaves, tomatoes, cucumber and olives.

4-5 WHOLE CORIANDER SEEDS
I teaspoon SALT
2 teaspoons MINT, CHOPPED
I teaspoon DILL, CHOPPED
3 tablespoons OLIVE OIL
JUICE OF HALF A LEMON

Grind the coriander seeds with the salt using a pestle and mortar. When the seeds are crushed, add the herbs and grind again. Beat in first the oil and lemon juice, then the coriander and herb mixture.

GREEK SALAD DRESSING

Serve on a salad of green leaves, tomatoes, cucumber, black olives and crumbled *Feta* cheese.

4 tablespoons OLIVE OIL
JUICE OF I LEMON
I teaspoon OREGANO OR WINTER SAVORY, CHOPPED
I teaspoon PARSLEY, CHOPPED
SALT AND BLACK PEPPER

Place all the ingredients in a container and beat well with a fork to form an emulsion. Use at once.

CUMIN DRESSING FOR MUSHROOMS

This unusual Spanish dressing probably originated among the Arabs who conquered Spain during the Middle Ages.

100ml/4fl oz/½ cup EXTRA VIRGIN OLIVE OIL
4 tablespoons FRESH LEMON JUICE
2 cloves GARLIC, CRUSHED
2½ tablespoons PARSLEY, CHOPPED
½ teaspoon GROUND CUMIN
SALT AND BLACK PEPPER

Place all the ingredients in a container and whisk with a fork to obtain an emulsion. Pour over sliced mushrooms and leave to stand for an hour before serving.

Makes sufficient for 350g/12oz mushrooms.

RAVIGOTE SAUCE

This cold French sauce sometimes has a chopped hard-boiled egg added to it.

125ml/5fl oz/⅔ cup OLIVE OIL
2 tablespoons RED WINE VINEGAR
1 tablespoon SHALLOTS OR SPRING ONIONS, FINELY CHOPPED
2 teaspoons CAPERS, CHOPPED
1 tablespoon each CHIVES, PARSLEY AND CHERVIL, ALL CHOPPED
1 teaspoon TARRAGON, CHOPPED
SALT AND PEPPER

Whisk the oil and vinegar together and fold in all the remaining ingredients. Use at once.

FRENCH CREAM DRESSING

In France this dressing is traditionally used on cabbage-based salads, on romaine or cos lettuce and on salsify.

4 tablespoons FRESH WHIPPING OR (RUNNY) DOUBLE CREAM
1 tablespoon WHITE WINE VINEGAR
SALT AND PEPPER

Place all the ingredients in a container and whisk well. Use the dressing at once.

Variation

■ Add ½ teaspoon Dijon mustard or 1 teaspoon whole-grain Meaux mustard.

LOW-FAT BLUE CHEESE DRESSING

75g/3oz/¾ cup BLUE CHEESE (ROQUEFORT, STILTON OR GORGONZOLA)
4 tablespoons FROMAGE FRAIS, QUARK OR LOW-FAT SOFT CHEESE
1 tablespoon OLIVE OIL
1 tablespoon WHITE WINE VINEGAR
3-4 tablespoons SKIMMED MILK

Place all the ingredients in a blender or food processor and blend until smooth and creamy.

Blue Cheese Dressing

This dressing comes from Lombardy in Italy. It is particularly good served with a lettuce and walnut salad.

100g/4oz/1 cup **GORGONZOLA CHEESE**
50ml/2fl oz/¼ cup **VIRGIN OLIVE OIL**
1½ tablespoons **WHITE WINE VINEGAR**
3 tablespoons **SINGLE CREAM**
1 clove **GARLIC, CRUSHED**
1 teaspoon **TARRAGON, CHOPPED**

Mash the *Gorgonzola* with a fork or in a food processor. Gradually add the oil and then the vinegar, beating all the time. Then add the cream, garlic and tarragon to produce a smooth, creamy dressing.

Rich Roquefort Dressing

50g/2oz/½ cup **ROQUEFORT CHEESE, DICED**
6 tablespoons **OLIVE OIL**
1 tablespoon **SHERRY VINEGAR**
BLACK PEPPER
1-2 tablespoons **MILK**

Place all the ingredients except the milk in a blender or food processor and blend until smooth. Add a little milk to the dressing to give a creamy consistency.

Sorrel Sauce

The slightly bitter leaves of wild sorrel were popular in medieval England and often appear in traditional sauces.

100g/4oz/1 cup **SORREL LEAVES, FINELY CHOPPED**
225g/9oz/2 cups **COX'S ORANGE PIPPIN APPLES, CORED AND DICED**
125ml/5fl oz/⅔ cup **CIDER VINEGAR**
25g/1oz/⅛ cup **SUGAR**
25g/1oz/⅛ cup **BUTTER**

Put the sorrel and apples in a pan with the vinegar and bring to the boil. Cook for 8-10 minutes until the apples are soft. Purée in a blender or food processor, or rub through a sieve. Return to a gentle heat, stir in the sugar and butter, and continue to stir until they have dissolved. The sauce can be served hot or cold.

HARISSA

This hot chilli sauce from North Africa will keep for quite a while in the fridge. Use sparingly in soups and stews and with *Couscous*.

100g/4oz/½ cup **DRIED RED CHILLI PEPPERS, TRIMMED AND SEEDED**
4 cloves **GARLIC**
1 teaspoon **SEA SALT**
125ml/5fl oz/⅔ cup **OLIVE OIL**

Soak the seeded chilli peppers in warm water for about an hour until they soften. Drain and grind to a paste in a mortar with the garlic and salt. Alternatively process in a food processor and then add the olive oil in a slow trickle to give a smooth sauce.

PIRI-PIRI SAUCE

This Portuguese sauce can be used for frying whole prawns in their shells, basting chicken or pouring over grilled meats. Go easy with it as it is pretty strong. It is similar to a flavoured olive oil used in the South of France for pouring over pizzas, though the latter also includes garlic.

DRIED RED CHILLI PEPPERS
OLIVE OIL

Place some dried red chilli peppers in a jar. (The Portuguese fill the jar about a third full, which makes a very strongly-flavoured oil.) Fill up with olive oil and leave to stand for a week or so before using.

Variation

■ Add some cloves of garlic to the red peppers.

XATO SAUCE

This Spanish sauce is often served on tuna salad. The almonds help the oil and vinegar to form a thick emulsion rather like mayonnaise.

125g/5oz/1¼ cups **GROUND ALMONDS**
1 **SMALL RED PEPPER**
2 large cloves **GARLIC, CRUSHED**
2 tablespoons **PARSLEY, CHOPPED**
SALT AND PEPPER

75ml/3fl oz/⅓ cup RED WINE VINEGAR
150ml/6fl oz/¾ cup OLIVE OIL
2½ tablespoons BOILING WATER

Grill the ground almonds until they turn pale gold. Then grill the red pepper, peel it, remove the seeds and chop it. Place the almonds and red pepper in a blender or food processor and blend with the garlic, parsley, seasoning and vinegar. With the motor still running, add the olive oil very slowly and finally the boiling water.

GREEN SAUCE

A version of this sauce was first published in England during the 15th century and very little has changed in the recipe since then. It was originally served as a sauce for boiled meat or poultry, but it is just as good used with hot or cold roast meats. It is also effective poured over a simple leaf salad, which can be served either as a side salad or as a starter to a meal.

2 tablespoons PARSLEY, CHOPPED
1 tablespoon CHIVES, CHOPPED
1 tablespoon MINT, CHOPPED
1 clove GARLIC, CRUSHED
1 teaspoon TARRAGON, CHOPPED
1 teaspoon CHERVIL, CHOPPED
50ml/2fl oz/¼ cup OLIVE OIL
2 tablespoons WHITE WINE VINEGAR
1 tablespoon LEMON JUICE
SALT AND PEPPER

Mix all the herbs together in a bowl. Gradually blend in the oil; then add the vinegar and lemon juice.

SHERRY DRESSING

Not surprisingly this dressing comes from Jerez, the home of sherry. It is usually served on salads of grated carrot or shredded greens.

2 tablespoons AMONTILLADO SHERRY
2 tablespoons SHERRY VINEGAR
1 teaspoon DIJON MUSTARD
SALT AND PEPPER

Mix all the ingredients thoroughly.

HONEY DRESSING

This hot dressing goes well with prawn or scallop salads.

4 tablespoons WHITE WINE VINEGAR
1½ teaspoons CLEAR HONEY

Heat the vinegar and honey in a small saucepan and stir until the honey dissolves. Pour the hot sauce over the salad.

MAYONNAISE AND EGG-BASED DRESSINGS

Mayonnaise is a traditional French dressing, which is made from an emulsion of raw egg yolk and oil, flavoured with lemon juice or vinegar and seasoning.

In 17th-century England a similar sauce was extremely popular for salads, but it used a hard-boiled egg yolk beaten with a classic vinaigrette. A number of hard-boiled egg-based sauces still survive.

In all of these sauces, the quality of the ingredients is again the important factor. The actual types of oils, vinegars and flavourings used are as much a matter of personal taste as they are for simple oil and vinegar dressings.

MAYONNAISE

The classic proportions for mayonnaise are one-third of a pint or 200ml olive oil to 1 medium egg yolk.

3 MEDIUM EGG YOLKS
1 tablespoon VINEGAR OR LEMON JUICE
1 teaspoon SALT
1 pinch WHITE PEPPER
600ml/1 pint/2½ cups OLIVE OIL

Put the egg yolks in a bowl with a little of the vinegar and the salt and pepper. Whisk gently together. Continue to whisk as you add the oil, a drop at a time to start with and then in a trickle. Add a little more vinegar from time to time. Continue until all the oil has been absorbed. The recipe makes a thick mayonnaise which can be thinned by adding 3 tablespoons boiling water; this also helps to preserve the texture if it is to be stored for some time.
Variation
■ Replace some of the olive oil with nut oil. Mayonnaise made solely with nut oil has a very strong flavour – perhaps

too strong for some. This is also true of mayonnaise made with extra virgin olive oil, though it is popular in countries where olives are grown.

Notes

■ Use oil and eggs which are at room temperature. Do not take eggs directly from the fridge, nor use oil which has started to thicken and turn opaque as a result of being stored in a cold place.

■ Mayonnaise which separates during preparation can be saved by the following procedure. Pour all but 1 tablespoon of the mayonnaise into another container. Add 1 tablespoon of water to the bowl and whisk. Continue to whisk as you gradually add the separated mayonnaise. The mixture should begin to cohere; if it does not, repeat the process. This is most successful if a blender is used.

WHOLE-EGG MAYONNAISE I

Mayonnaise made with a whole egg is much lighter and less rich than the classic recipe.

I MEDIUM EGG
300ml/½ pint/1¼ cups OLIVE OIL
I tablespoon WHITE WINE VINEGAR OR LEMON JUICE
SALT AND PEPPER

Whisk the egg with a wire or an electric whisk. Gradually beat in the oil, pouring it in a steady stream. Finally add vinegar or lemon juice to taste.

WHOLE-EGG MAYONNAISE II

This is a slightly richer version than the recipe above.

I MEDIUM EGG
I MEDIUM EGG YOLK
350ml/12fl oz/1½ cups OLIVE OIL
I tablespoon WINE VINEGAR OR LEMON JUICE

Whisk the egg with a wire or an electric whisk. Gradually beat in the oil, pouring it in a steady stream.

Variations

Many other flavourings can be added to create variations on any of the above recipes for mayonnaise. Here are a number of possible additions to a quantity of 300ml/½pt/1¼ cups mayonnaise:

■ Add 1 teaspoon Dijon mustard.

■ Add 2 teaspoons capers, drained and chopped.

- Add 1 tablespoon red or black lumpfish roe.
- Add 1 tablespoon tarragon, chopped.
- Add 1 tablespoon shallots, finely chopped.
- Add 1 teaspoon mild *garam masala* or curry powder.
- Add 1 tablespoon chutney, chopped.
- Add 1 tablespoon tomato purée plus 2 tablespoons basil, chopped, and a dash of Tabasco sauce.
- Add 2 tablespoons olive paste.
- Use raspberry, herb or any other flavoured vinegar.
- Use lime juice in place of vinegar plus 1 tablespoon coriander, chopped.

FRENCH GREEN MAYONNAISE

2-3 leaves SPINACH
4-5 sprigs WATERCRESS
A few sprigs each PARSLEY, CHERVIL AND TARRAGON
300ml/½ pint/1¼ cups MAYONNAISE (see pages 100-01)

Place the herbs in boiling water. Drain and refresh in cold water. Then drain again and dry well. Pound in a mortar and stir the herbs into the mayonnaise.

SPANISH GREEN MAYONNAISE

3-4 leaves SPINACH, SHREDDED
5-6 sprigs PARSLEY, CHOPPED
1 teaspoon MINT, CHOPPED
200ml/8fl oz/1 cup MAYONNAISE (see pages 100-01)

Chop the herbs and spinach leaves finely, preferably in a food processor, and fold into the mayonnaise.
Variation
- Add 1 tablespoon pistachio nuts, chopped.

GERMAN GREEN MAYONNAISE

3 tablespoons PARSLEY, CHOPPED
3 tablespoons CHERVIL, CHOPPED
2 tablespoons BASIL, CHOPPED
½ teaspoon ROSEMARY, CHOPPED
200ml/8fl oz/1 cup MAYONNAISE (see pages 100-01)
50ml/2fl oz/¼ cup QUARK OR LOW-FAT CHEESE

Mix all the ingredients thoroughly.
Variation
- Add 2 small pickled gherkins, very finely chopped.

RECIPES

AIOLI

This cold garlic sauce is a favourite in the South of France, where it is known as *Beurre de Provence*.

I EGG YOLK
5 cloves GARLIC, CRUSHED
SALT
200ml/8fl oz/I cup OLIVE OIL
I teaspoon LEMON JUICE
1-2 teaspoons WATER

Mix the egg yolk, garlic and salt; then pour in the oil slowly, whisking all the time. Add the lemon juice and a little water. Leave overnight in the fridge for the best flavour.

ALLIOLI

This Spanish version of cold garlic sauce is served with new potatoes and fish stews.

I EGG
6 cloves GARLIC, CRUSHED
100ml/4fl oz/½ cup EXTRA VIRGIN OLIVE OIL
200ml/8fl oz/I cup OLIVE, SUNFLOWER OR GROUND-NUT OIL
I tablespoon LEMON JUICE

Mix the egg, garlic and salt, and pour in the oil very slowly, whisking all the time. Then add the lemon juice and a little water. Leave in the fridge overnight for best results.

SAUCE ROUILLE

This garlic and pepper sauce is traditionally spread on hard French bread croutons for *Bouillabaisse*.

JUICE OF HALF A LEMON
4-5 strands SAFFRON
I EGG YOLK
6 cloves GARLIC, CRUSHED
SALT
I teaspoon CHILLI POWDER (OR TO TASTE)
200ml/8fl oz/I cup OLIVE OIL

Soak the saffron in the lemon juice for at least half an hour. Mix the egg yolk, garlic and chilli in a bowl and gradually add the oil, a little at a time. Finally, beat in the lemon juice and saffron.

Sauce Dijonnaise

This is a classic recipe from Burgundy.

4 HARD-BOILED EGG YOLKS
1½ tablespoons DIJON MUSTARD
JUICE OF 1 LEMON
200ml/8fl oz/1 cup OLIVE OIL
SALT AND PEPPER

Sieve or mash the egg yolks finely and mix into a paste with the mustard. Gradually beat in the lemon juice. Whisk the mixture with a wire whisk and add the oil in a thin but steady trickle. Season with salt and pepper.

Iranian Salad Dressing

This dressing is often used to dress cooked vegetables and can also be used to make Russian mixed vegetable salad.

75ml/3fl oz/⅓ cup MAYONNAISE (see pages 100-01)
50ml/2fl oz/¼ cup SOURED CREAM OR THICK YOGHURT
3 tablespoons OLIVE OIL
1 tablespoon LEMON JUICE
½ teaspoon DRY MUSTARD
SALT AND PEPPER

Mix the mayonnaise with the soured cream or yoghurt. Beat the oil and lemon juice together with the mustard and seasoning. Then pour it into the mayonnaise mixture and beat together with a fork.

Thousand Island Dressing

This is an extremely popular dressing in the USA. The home-made version is much pleasanter than those normally encountered in restaurants and bottles.

200ml/8fl oz/1 cup MAYONNAISE (see pages 100-01)
3 tablespoons CHILLI SAUCE OR TOMATO KETCHUP
1 tablespoon GREEN PEPPER, FINELY CHOPPED
1 tablespoon CHIVES OR SPRING ONION, FINELY CHOPPED
2 tablespoons STUFFED OLIVES, FINELY CHOPPED
1 HARD-BOILED EGG, CHOPPED
2 teaspoons PARSLEY, CHOPPED

Place all the ingredients in a bowl and mix well. Store the finished dressing in the fridge.

AMERICAN GREEN GODDESS DRESSING

100ml/4fl oz/½ cup MAYONNAISE (see pages 100-01)
50ml/2fl oz/¼ cup SOURED CREAM
2 MINCED ANCHOVY FILLETS OR ½ tablespoon ANCHOVY ESSENCE
½ clove GARLIC, CRUSHED
2 tablespoons CHIVES OR SPRING ONIONS, CHOPPED
2 tablespoons PARSLEY, CHOPPED
2 teaspoons LEMON JUICE
SALT AND PEPPER

Place all the ingredients in a bowl and mix well. Store the finished dressing in the fridge.

PRAWN COCKTAIL SAUCE

The universally popular prawn cocktail was invented by the Americans. Here's how to make the sauce:

125ml/5fl oz/⅔ cup MAYONNAISE (see pages 100-01)
3-4 tablespoons TOMATO KETCHUP, OR TO TASTE
1 tablespoon GRATED HORSERADISH
1 teaspoon WORCESTERSHIRE SAUCE
LEMON JUICE TO TASTE

Mix the mayonnaise and tomato ketchup to taste. Then stir in all the remaining ingredients, using the lemon juice for flavour and to thin the sauce.

ORIENTAL MAYONNAISE

This was inspired by a sesame mayonnaise from the Silver Palate Gourmet Food Shop in New York.

1 WHOLE EGG
2 EGG YOLKS
2 tablespoons RICE VINEGAR
2 tablespoons LIGHT SOY SAUCE
2 tablespoons DIJON MUSTARD
50ml/2fl oz/¼ cup ROASTED SESAME OIL
600ml/1 pint/2½ cups CORN OR SUNFLOWER OIL

Mix the egg, egg yolks, vinegar, soy sauce and mustard in a blender or food processor. With the motor still running, pour in the oils in a very thin trickle.

This recipe makes quite a large quantity of mayonnaise, but it will store in the fridge for a week or so.

Variations

■ Add a little freshly-grated orange rind.

■ Add a little Szechwan-style hot pepper or hot spicy oil.

REMOULADE SAUCE I

This classic sauce is made by adding herbs and pickles to a basic mayonnaise.

I tablespoon DIJON MUSTARD
½ teaspoon ANCHOVY ESSENCE
I tablespoon GHERKINS, CHOPPED
I teaspoon CAPERS, CHOPPED
I tablespoon PARSLEY, CHOPPED
I tablespoon CHERVIL, CHOPPED
300ml/½ pint/1¼ cups MAYONNAISE (see pages 100-01)

Fold all the other ingredients carefully into the mayonnaise.

REMOULADE SAUCE II

This sauce can also be made with hard-boiled eggs. If the oil is beaten into the mashed egg yolks, a consistency similar to mayonnaise will be achieved. Alternatively, the oil and vinegar may be beaten together and the eggs added later. This results in a much thinner sauce.

3 HARD-BOILED EGGS
300ml/½ pint/1¼ cups OLIVE OIL
2 tablespoons WINE VINEGAR
I tablespoon GHERKINS, CHOPPED
I teaspoon CAPERS, CHOPPED
I tablespoon PARSLEY, CHOPPED
I tablespoon CHERVIL, CHOPPED
SALT AND PEPPER

Mash the egg yolks and chop the egg whites. Mix the yolks with a little oil to form a smooth paste and then gradually beat in the rest of the oil. Finally, fold in all the remaining ingredients of the sauce.

GIBRICHE SAUCE

This sauce is usually served with fish, shellfish or pigs' trotters. It is also very good poured on a salad of chickpeas or *haricot* beans. Garlic is sometimes added. The sauce can be served either hot or cold.

4 HARD-BOILED EGGS, SEPARATED
125ml/5fl oz/⅔ cup OLIVE OIL
3 tablespoons WHITE WINE VINEGAR
I teaspoon TARRAGON, CHERVIL AND PARSLEY, ALL CHOPPED
I teaspoon CAPERS, CHOPPED
I teaspoon GHERKINS, CHOPPED
I SPRING ONION, CHOPPED
SALT AND PEPPER

Place the egg yolks in a blender or mash thoroughly with a fork. Very slowly add the oil, beating all the time. Next add the vinegar and fold in the remaining ingredients.

Variation

■ Add 1 teaspoon Dijon mustard.
■ Add 1 clove garlic, crushed.

SAUCE TARTARE

The classic *Sauce Tartare* was made with hard-boiled egg yolks. Today it is more often made with a standard raw egg yolk mayonnaise. This recipe offers a combination of the two methods, which is less rich and less heavy than the mayonnaise-based sauce, but which holds together longer than the classic recipe.

2 HARD-BOILED EGG YOLKS
I teaspoon WINE VINEGAR OR LEMON JUICE
I RAW EGG YOLK
SALT AND PEPPER
200ml/8fl oz/I cup OLIVE OIL
I teaspoon each TARRAGON, CHIVES AND CHERVIL, ALL CHOPPED
I teaspoon CAPERS, CHOPPED

Sieve or mash the hard-boiled egg yolks with the vinegar or lemon juice and mix to a paste. Beat in the raw egg yolk and seasoning. Gradually add the oil in a thin stream, whisking all the time. When it is thick and smooth, stir in the chopped herbs and capers.

Variations

■ Add 1 teaspoon Dijon mustard to the mixture.
■ To revert to the classic recipe, use 3 hard-boiled egg yolks and omit the raw egg yolk. In theory you should also omit the tarragon, chervil and capers.

■ If you prefer to use the standard mayonnaise instead, add the same quantities of herbs and capers to 200ml/8fl oz/ 1 cup mayonnaise.

■ We came across an amusing variation of *Sauce Tartare* in a book on American Cajun cooking. It is a good recipe for a spicy mayonnaise, but doesn't seem to have much relevance to the original!

200ml/8fl oz/1 cup MAYONNAISE (see pages 100-01)
JUICE OF 1½ LEMONS
1 tablespoon SWEET PICKLE RELISH
3-4 drops TABASCO SAUCE

Mix all the ingredients together and thin with a little wine vinegar if desired.

SALPICON SAUCE

This is a Spanish sauce which is particularly good served with fish or shellfish.

100ml/4fl oz/½ cup OLIVE OIL
50ml/2fl oz/¼ cup RED WINE VINEGAR
1 SMALL ONION, MINCED
4 GHERKINS, CHOPPED
4 teaspoons CAPERS, CHOPPED
1 HARD-BOILED EGG, FINELY CHOPPED
1 tablespoon PARSLEY, CHOPPED
SALT AND PEPPER

Whisk the oil and vinegar together and fold in the remaining ingredients.

Variation

■ Add 1 teaspoon mustard to the above recipe.

MARINADES

Marinades are generally used to tenderize cuts of meat which might otherwise be tough, or to make possible faster methods of cooking. They may also be used to moisten and flavour meat or fish.

Most marinades include an acidic ingredient like vinegar which helps to break down the tough cell structure of the meat. The vinegar also helps to retard the growth and activity of the micro-organisms which cause food spoilage and decay. This means that perishable foods will keep for longer if they are in a marinade.

The flavouring elements of a marinade may come only from the vinegar and oils used, but they will probably also include mustards, herbs and spices. Marinade ingredients should be mixed well and poured over the food. Stir or turn the food in the marinade at regular intervals.

RED WINE MARINADE FOR BEEF AND GAME

600ml/1 pint/2½ cups RED OR WHITE WINE
150ml/6fl oz/¾ cup RED OR WHITE WINE VINEGAR
50ml/2fl oz/¼ cup OLIVE OR OTHER OIL
1 SMALL ONION, CHOPPED
2 CARROTS, DICED
1 stick CELERY, CHOPPED
½ teaspoon BLACK PEPPERCORNS
1 clove GARLIC
1 BAYLEAF
½ teaspoon each DRIED THYME AND OREGANO
SALT

Allow at least 12 hours. Roast or casserole the meat.
Variation
■ Add 1 clove of garlic, crushed.

JUNIPER MARINADE FOR VENISON

300ml/½ pint/1¼ cups RED WINE
100ml/4fl oz/½ cup RED WINE VINEGAR
100ml/4fl oz/½ cup OLIVE OR OTHER OIL
1 SMALL ONION, CHOPPED
1 CARROT, CHOPPED
2 stalks CELERY, CHOPPED
1 clove GARLIC, CHOPPED
1 BOUQUET GARNI
6 JUNIPER BERRIES, CRUSHED
6 WHOLE CORIANDER SEEDS, CRUSHED
6 WHOLE PEPPERCORNS
SALT AND PEPPER

Allow at least 24 hours. Roast or casserole the meat.
Variation
■ Add 1 tablespoon brandy to the marinade.

LEMON MARINADE FOR VENISON

300ml/½ pint/1¼ cups RED OR WHITE WINE
300ml/½ pint/1¼ cups RED OR WHITE WINE VINEGAR
300ml/½ pint/1¼ cups OLIVE OR OTHER OIL
12 PEPPERCORNS
2 BAYLEAVES
1 LEMON, SLICED
2 sprigs THYME
SALT

Allow at least 24 hours. Roast or casserole the meat.

GINGER AND SHERRY MARINADE FOR CHICKEN OR TURKEY

100ml/4fl oz/½ cup SOY SAUCE
2 tablespoons SHERRY VINEGAR
1 tablespoon SWEET SHERRY
1 tablespoon OLIVE OR OTHER OIL
1 clove GARLIC, CRUSHED
1 tablespoon ROOT GINGER, FINELY GRATED

Allow at least 1 hour. Grill the meat or bake in foil.

CURRY MARINADE FOR CHICKEN OR TURKEY

100ml/4fl oz/½ cup OLIVE OIL
75ml/3fl oz/⅓ cup WHITE WINE VINEGAR
1 teaspoon GARAM MASALA OR CURRY POWDER
1 clove GARLIC, CRUSHED
SALT AND PEPPER

Allow at least 2 hours. Grill or barbecue the meat.

MARINADE FOR SAUERBRATEN

Sauerbraten is served in Germany as a special dish for weddings, birthdays and other family gatherings. It generally uses beef.

600ml/1 pint/2½ cups RED WINE
300ml/½ pint/1¼ cups RED WINE VINEGAR

2 ONIONS, PEELED AND SLICED
6 WHOLE PEPPERCORNS
6 JUNIPER BERRIES
3 cloves GARLIC, CRUSHED
I BAYLEAF
SALT

Allow at least 3 days. Pot-roast the meat very slowly.

MARINADE FOR COOKED CARP OR HERRING

This is a central European marinade for fried fillets of fish.

100ml/4fl oz/½ cup WATER
125ml/5fl oz/⅔ cup MALT VINEGAR
I BAYLEAF
6 PEPPERCORNS
3 teaspoons SALT
LEMON RIND

Place all the ingredients in a pan and bring to the boil. Reduce the heat and simmer for 30 minutes. Leave to cool before pouring over the cooked fish. Allow to stand for at least 1 hour.

ESCABECHE MARINADE FOR COOKED FISH

This is a Spanish marinade for cooked fish such as sardines, cod fillets and herring.

100ml/4fl oz/½ cup OLIVE OIL
5 cloves GARLIC
150ml/6fl oz/¾ cup RED OR WHITE WINE VINEGAR
150ml/6fl oz/¾ cup DRY WHITE WINE
100ml/4fl oz/½ cup FISH STOCK
2 BAYLEAVES
6 PEPPERCORNS
I LEMON, SLICED

Heat the oil in a pan and fry the garlic until golden. Add all the remaining ingredients except the lemon and bring to the boil. Reduce by half and pour over the cooked fish. Arrange the lemon slices on top. Allow the marinade to stand for at least 2 days. Serve at room temperature.

SWEDISH MARINADE FOR RAW HERRING OR SPRATT FILLETS

6 tablespoons OLIVE OR OTHER OIL
3 tablespoons WHITE WINE VINEGAR
I tablespoon MILD MUSTARD
3 WHITE PEPPERCORNS
I tablespoon SUGAR
I teaspoon SALT

Allow to stand for at least 6 hours.

Variations

■ Add 6 whole allspice, crushed, and a little dill.

■ Add sugar.

PICKLES

Pickles rely on the preserving qualities of vinegar. Sometimes, vegetables are pickled as they are; sometimes, they are salted before pickling to remove any excess water which might dilute the vinegar. In either case, the quality of the vinegar is important: it must have an acetic acid content of at least five per cent. Most commercial vinegars reach this level, but vinegar bought from a barrel may not.

Pickling vinegar is usually spiced. Ideally, spiced vinegar should be made a week or two in advance of pickling in order to allow the flavours to mix thoroughly beforehand, but this process can be speeded up by heating the ingredients together. The end result will not be quite so good, but it will be acceptable.

Malt vinegar is the vinegar most commonly used for pickles, but cider and wine vinegar produce a more delicate flavour. Malt vinegar needs quite heavy spicing. White vinegar shows off the pickles to best advantage, but it has less flavour. White wine vinegar is light enough for most purposes and it needs less spice than malt vinegar.

In addition to using top-quality vinegar, you should also buy fresh whole spices. Spices which have been hanging around a cupboard or sitting in a shop for a year or more will not give the best results. It is wise to buy from a stockist who has a good turnover in spices.

Always use stainless steel, aluminium or unchipped enamel-coated cast iron for heating vinegar. Copper, iron and brass are unsuitable. Check that the lids of your containers are also vinegar-proof.

WELL-SPICED MALT VINEGAR

1½ litres/2½ pints/6 cups MALT VINEGAR

15g/½ oz each DRY ROOT GINGER, CINNAMON STICKS AND WHOLE ALLSPICE BERRIES

8g/¼ oz each WHOLE BLACK PEPPERCORNS AND WHOLE CLOVES

Stir the spices into the vinegar and leave to stand for 2-4 weeks. Use a larger quantity of vinegar if you wish. Shake once a week. If you prefer a clear vinegar, strain before use or place the spices in the vinegar inside a muslin parcel.

Variation

■ Use mace or mustard seed in place of root ginger.

SPICED WINE VINEGAR

1½ litres/2½ pints/6 cups WINE VINEGAR

8g/¼ oz each MUSTARD SEED, WHOLE ALLSPICE BERRIES AND MACE

4g/⅛ oz each CINNAMON STICKS AND WHOLE BLACK PEPPERCORNS

2-3 WHOLE CLOVES

Stir the spices into the vinegar, using a larger quantity if you wish, and leave to stand for 2-4 weeks. Shake once a week. If you prefer a clear vinegar, strain before use or place the spices in the vinegar inside a muslin parcel.

HERB VINEGARS

If you grow herbs in the garden it is easy to make your own herb vinegar. Pick the leaves of the chosen herb before it has flowered. Early morning is the best time to pick herbs because strong sun dries the oils on the leaf surface. Push the leaves into a jam jar until it is half-full, with the leaves slightly crushed. Cover them with cold vinegar and seal. Very strongly flavoured herbs like rosemary will be ready to use in 24 hours. Others may take up to 2 weeks.

LEMON AND ORANGE VINEGAR

Carefully peel the rind off the fruit, leaving behind the pith. Dry the rind in a cool oven for about 1 hour; then place in a jam jar, cover with cold vinegar and seal. The more rind you use, the stronger the flavour will be. Start with the rind of one fruit in one jar.

CHILLI VINEGAR

6 FRESH GREEN CHILLIES
600ml/1 pint/2½ cups **VINEGAR**

Roughly chop the chillies and place them in a jar. Bring the vinegar to the boil. Pour over the chillies and leave to cool. Cover and leave for 3 weeks. Strain and re-bottle.

Variation

■ Use 225g/8oz celery or shallots in place of chillies for celery or shallot vinegar.

HORSERADISH VINEGAR

It is hard to beat this simple recipe from Mrs Beeton.

1.2 litres/2 pints/5 cups **RED WINE VINEGAR**
100g/4oz/¾ cup **GRATED HORSERADISH**
1 SMALL **SHALLOT**, VERY FINELY CHOPPED
1 pinch **CAYENNE PEPPER**

Put all the ingredients into a bottle and shake well every day for a fortnight. Strain, bottle and use as required.

SWEET PICKLING VINEGAR

Some kinds of food, like fruit, are good pickled in sweet pickling vinegar.

1½ litres/2½ pints/6 cups **WINE VINEGAR**
450g/1lb/2 cups **SUGAR**
8g/¼ oz each **DRIED ROOT GINGER, WHOLE ALLSPICE BERRIES AND MACE**
4g/⅛oz **CINNAMON STICKS**
2-3 WHOLE **CLOVES**

Use a larger quantity of vinegar if you wish.

MUSTARD PICKLES

600ml/1 pint/2½ cups **SPICED VINEGAR**
100g/4oz/⅔ cup **DRY MUSTARD**
100g/4oz/⅔ cup **CORNFLOUR**
1 teaspoon **TURMERIC**
1-2 DRIED RED **CHILLIES**

Mix a small quantity of the vinegar with the mustard and cornflour to form a smooth paste. Stir in the rest of the vinegar and pour into a saucepan. Gradually bring to the boil, stirring all the time. When the mixture thickens, stir in the remaining ingredients. Use as spiced vinegar.

SOFTENING AND BRINING PICKLED ONIONS

Unless the onions chosen for pickling are very small indeed, they will need to be softened. If they are to be kept for some time they may also need to be salted.

Softening
Large pickling onions for immediate use can either be soaked in cold water for 2 hours, or they can be placed in a saucepan of cold water and brought to the boil. Drain and cool slightly before use.

Brining
Place the onions in a bowl in layers. Sprinkle each layer with a coarse, dry salt. Never use cooking salt for brining; the added chemicals can affect the pickling vinegar. Allow about 100g/4oz/⅓ cup salt to every 750g/1½lbs prepared vegetables. Cover with a cloth and leave to stand in a cool place overnight. Drain and rinse under cold running water. Then rinse and drain thoroughly again.

ENGLISH PICKLED ONIONS

1kg/2lb PREPARED PICKLING ONIONS, BRINED OR SOAKED
1.2 litres/2 pints/5 cups WELL-SPICED MALT VINEGAR

Pack the onions into a jar and cover them with the spiced vinegar. Seal the jar and leave for at least 2 weeks.

MIDDLE EASTERN PICKLED ONIONS I

1kg/2lb PREPARED PICKLING ONIONS, SOAKED
4 cloves GARLIC, CHOPPED
A few sprigs MINT
3 tablespoons SALT
1.2 litres/2 pints/5 cups WHITE WINE VINEGAR

Pack the onions into a jar, sprinkling with the garlic, mint and salt as you go. Cover with vinegar and seal.

MIDDLE EASTERN PICKLED ONIONS II

1 kg/2lb PREPARED PICKLING ONIONS, BRINED
4 tablespoons DARK MUSCOVADO SUGAR
1.2 litres/2 pints/5 cups WHITE WINE VINEGAR

Pack the onions into a jar, sprinkling with sugar as you go. Cover with vinegar and seal.

PICKLED RED CABBAGE

1 RED CABBAGE, FINELY SHREDDED
1 ONION, SLICED
COARSE SALT
1 tablespoon DARK MUSCOVADO SUGAR (OPTIONAL)
SPICED WINE VINEGAR

Place the cabbage and onion in a bowl in layers, sprinkling with salt as you go. Allow 100g/4oz/⅓ cup salt to each 450g/1lb cabbage. Cover and leave to stand overnight. Drain and wash under cold running water. Then drain again and pack into jars with the sugar, if using. Cover with spiced vinegar. Seal and leave for at least 2 weeks.

PICKLED CUCUMBERS

1 kg/2lb RIDGE OR SMALL MIDDLE EASTERN CUCUMBERS, TRIMMED
1.2 litres/2 pints/5 cups WATER
150g/6oz/¾ cup SALT
50g/2oz/¼ cup SUGAR
1.2 litres/2 pints/5 cups SPICED VINEGAR
BAYLEAVES

Cut the cucumbers into quarters lengthways. Boil the water and salt together and leave to cool. When the salted water is completely cold, pour over the cucumber. Leave to stand for 24 hours.

Put the sugar and spiced vinegar into a pan and heat gently until the sugar dissolves. Leave to cool. Remove the cucumber from the brine and wash under cold running water. Drain and leave to dry for 2 hours. Place in jars and cover with cold vinegar syrup. Add a bayleaf or two to each jar and seal. Keep 2-3 weeks before using.

PICKLED BEETROOT

1kg/2lb BEETROOT
1.2 litres/2 pints/5 cups SPICED MALT OR WINE VINEGAR
1 teaspoon SALT

Cook the beetroot in boiling water for 45 minutes to 1 hour, depending on size. Leave to cool. Then peel, slice and pack into jars. Mix the salt with the vinegar and pour over the top. Seal and use after 2-3 weeks.

Variation

■ Add a little horseradish to the spiced vinegar.

PICKLED EGGS

12 HARD-BOILED EGGS
1.2 litres/2 pints/5 cups SPICED WINE VINEGAR
15g/½oz each DRIED ROOT GINGER, MUSTARD SEEDS AND WHOLE PEPPERCORNS
2 DRIED CHILLIS

Place the eggs in a large jar. Pour the vinegar into a pan and add the spices. Bring to the boil and leave to cool. Pour over the eggs and leave for 2-3 weeks before eating.

PICKLED HERRING

1 large SALT HERRING, CLEANED, FILLETED AND SKINNED
400ml/16fl oz/2 cups WHITE WINE VINEGAR
75g/3oz/⅓ cup SUGAR
5-6 WHOLE PEPPERCORNS
5-6 WHOLE ALLSPICE
1 BAYLEAF
GARNISH OF 1 SMALL ONION, CUT INTO RINGS, AND 1 teaspoon WHOLE ALLSPICE, CRUSHED

Rinse the herring in lukewarm water and then soak in plenty of water for 6-7 hours. Drain on kitchen paper and remove as many small bones as possible. Cut into pieces diagonally and arrange in rows in a shallow dish. Mix all the remaining ingredients in a saucepan and bring to the boil. Cool, chill and pour over the herring. Leave in the fridge overnight. Serve garnished with onion rings and crushed allspice as part of a cold hors-d'oeuvre.

GENERAL RECIPES

The best ingredients, of course, produce the best dishes and will do so without too much effort on the part of the cook. All that is needed is careful cooking and a dash or two of the right flavouring or seasoning. Although most people will probably be willing to spend time on special meals, for everyday cooking they are looking for quick ways of making their food interesting and enjoyable.

There are plenty of popular relishes, piquant sauces and aids for making gravy and meat sauce on the market, but – good as many of them are – they do tend to make every meal taste the same. In this section we offer some general ideas to bring more individuality to cooking. Many of these are open to experimentation.

ANCHOVY AND GARLIC SPREAD

Serve on toasted bread, or use on canapés or as a stuffing for eggs, mushrooms and celery.

2 × 45g/1½oz cans ANCHOVY FILLETS, DRAINED AND CHOPPED
2 cloves GARLIC, CRUSHED
BLACK PEPPER, FRESHLY GROUND
¼ teaspoon DRIED THYME
6 tablespoons OLIVE OIL
2 tablespoons LEMON JUICE

Place the anchovies, garlic, pepper and thyme in a blender and process until smooth. Gradually add the oil and lemon juice alternately until the mixture forms a creamy paste.

BAGNA CAUDA

This famous speciality of Piedmont is eaten with celery, raw sliced cabbages and pimentos. Sometimes a sliced white truffle is added to the sauce.

75ml/3oz/⅓ cup OLIVE OIL
75g/3oz/⅓ cup BUTTER
75g/3oz/¾ cup GARLIC, SLICED
2 × 45g/1½oz cans ANCHOVY FILLETS, DRAINED AND CUT INTO PIECES

Heat the oil and butter in a pan. Then add the anchovies and garlic. Gently simmer for 10 minutes. Serve as a hot dip with the vegetables.

BRUSCHETTA

This makes a simple but delicious snack.

4 thick slices BREAD
I clove GARLIC
OLIVE OIL
SALT

Toast the bread, or bake it in the oven, and then rub it with the garlic. Sprinkle with plenty of olive oil and salt, and serve at once.

Variations

■ Finish off by sprinkling with minced truffles.

■ Finish off by spreading with sun-dried tomato paste.

PISTOU SAUCE FOR SOUP

This sauce is stirred into *Pistou*, the vegetable soup of Provence. A similar sauce is stirred into the Italian soup, *Minestrone alla Genovese*.

3 cloves GARLIC, CHOPPED
I bunch FRESH BASIL
50g/2oz/½ cup PARMESAN CHEESE, GRATED
2 tablespoons OLIVE OIL
SALT AND BLACK PEPPER

Grind the garlic and basil in a mortar or a food processor. Add the cheese and then the oil and seasoning. The mixture should be quite thick and stiff. Serve with the soup.

SHALLOT SAUCE

This simple French sauce is delicious served on hot steaks.

100g/4oz/½ cup BUTTER
150g/6oz SHALLOTS, CHOPPED
200ml/8fl oz/I cup VINEGAR
I large bunch PARSLEY, CHOPPED

Heat the butter in a pan and gently fry the shallots for about 2 minutes. Do not allow the shallots to brown. Add the vinegar and bring to the boil. Boil until the mixture has been reduced by half. Pour it into the pan used for cooking the steaks and add the parsley and seasoning. Stir well and pour over the steaks.

MUSTARD BUTTER

Serve on steaks, on lamb cutlets or on vegetables such as carrots and leeks.

125g/5oz/⅔ cup BUTTER
1½ tablespoons MUSTARD, TO TASTE
WHITE PEPPER
A few drops LEMON JUICE

Soften the butter but do not melt. Beat in the mustard, distributing it evenly. Season with the pepper and lemon juice. Roll the mixture into a sausage shape in greaseproof paper and chill until required. Cut into slices to serve.

Variation

■ Pat out the butter into a layer about ½cm/¼in thick between two layers of greaseproof paper. Chill flat. Cut into shapes or fluted rounds with a pastry cutter.

PESTO SAUCE FOR PASTA

1 large bunch BASIL
2-3 cloves GARLIC
½ teaspoon SEA SALT
25g/1oz/¼ cup PINENUTS
25g/1oz/¼ cup PARMESAN CHEESE, GRATED
50ml/2fl oz/¼ cup OLIVE OIL

Grind the basil and garlic with the salt and pinenuts in a mortar. Add the cheese and mix to a thick purée. Add the oil slowly, stirring steadily. When all the oil is added, the sauce should have a consistency of creamed butter.

Variation

■ In Genoa, a strongly-flavoured cheese called *Sardo* from Sardinia is sometimes used in the sauce with, or instead of, the *Parmesan* cheese.

BAGNAT SAUCE FOR PASTA

This sauce comes from Piedmont in north-western Italy.

1 large bunch PARSLEY
8 cloves GARLIC
100ml/4fl oz/½ cup OLIVE OIL

Place all the ingredients in a blender and process well. Store in a jar until required.

WALNUT AND PARSLEY SAUCE FOR PASTA

I small bunch PARSLEY
I clove GARLIC
½ teaspoon SALT
25g/1oz/¼ cup WALNUTS, CHOPPED
40g/1½oz/1⅓ cups PINENUTS
25ml/1fl oz/⅛ cup SINGLE OR LIGHT CREAM
125ml/5fl oz/⅔ cup WALNUT OIL
50g/2oz/¼ cup PECORINO CHEESE, GRATED

Place the parsley, garlic, salt and nuts in a blender. Add the cream and oil to process until smooth. Add the cheese and quickly blend again. Pour over cooked pasta and toss.

PASTA IN OLIVE CREAM SAUCE

450g/1lb DRIED PASTA
SALT
I teaspoon OLIVE OIL
600ml/1 pint/2½ cups DOUBLE OR HEAVY CREAM
4 tablespoons OLIVE PASTE

Cook the pasta in plenty of salted boiling water with the olive oil. Mix the cream and olive paste in a saucepan and bring to the boil. Drain the pasta and pour on the olive cream sauce.

Variation

■ This sauce is also very good with rice.

TAGLIATELLE WITH TRUFFLE AND ANCHOVY

1kg/2lb FRESH TAGLIATELLE
8 tablespoons OLIVE OIL
4 cloves GARLIC, THICKLY SLICED
4 ANCHOVIES, WASHED AND CHOPPED
4 tablespoons TOMATO PUREE
200ml/8fl oz/1 cup STOCK
2 TRUFFLES

Cook the *tagliatelle* in plenty of salted boiling water with 1 teaspoon olive oil. Fry the garlic in the remaining olive oil until brown; then remove it with a slotted spoon. Add the anchovies, tomato purée and stock to the oil and bring to the boil. Drain the cooked pasta and pour on the sauce. Grate the truffle over the top and toss well together.

ABRUZZO SAUCE FOR PASTA

This sauce comes from Abruzzi on the east coast of Italy.

4 tablespoons OLIVE OIL
4 cloves GARLIC
I HOT RED PEPPER

Heat the olive oil, and then fry the garlic and pepper until well-browned. Strain off the oil and use to toss spaghetti. Garnish with freshly-chopped parsley.

HUNGARIAN BEETROOT SALAD

700g/1½lb COOKED BEETROOT, PEELED AND SLICED
50ml/2fl oz/¼ cup RED WINE VINEGAR
I teaspoon SALT
¼ teaspoon CARAWAY SEEDS
I teaspoon HORSERADISH, GRATED
125ml/5fl oz/⅔ cup SAUCE TARTARE (see page 107)
GARNISH OF PARSLEY, FRESHLY CHOPPED

Place the slices of beetroot in a bowl. Mix the vinegar with the salt, caraway seeds and horseradish, and pour over the beetroot. Leave to stand for 3-4 hours, or overnight. Drain and cut the beetroot into strips. Mix with the *Sauce Tartare* and serve garnished with freshly-chopped parsley.

HAZELNUT POTATOES

Ikg/2lb POTATOES, SLICED
3 ONIONS, SLICED
SALT AND BLACK PEPPER
100ml/4fl oz/½ cup HAZELNUT OIL

Set the oven to 200°C/400°F/Gas Mark 6. Layer the potatoes and onions with the seasoning in a casserole dish. Bake for 45 minutes until the vegetables are cooked.
Variation
■ Use walnut oil in place of hazelnut oil.

MUSHROOMS IN GARLIC AND SHERRY VINEGAR

This Spanish recipe can be served hot or cold.

4 tablespoons **EXTRA VIRGIN OLIVE OIL**
450g/1lb **MUSHROOMS, THICKLY SLICED**
3 cloves **GARLIC, THINLY SLICED**
2 tablespoons **SHERRY VINEGAR**
50ml/2fl oz/¼ cup **STOCK**
2 teaspoons **LEMON JUICE**
½ teaspoon **HOT PAPRIKA**
¼ teaspoon **CHILLI POWDER**
SALT AND PEPPER
GARNISH OF PARSLEY, FRESHLY CHOPPED

Heat the oil, and then stir-fry the mushrooms and garlic over a high heat for 2 minutes. Lower the heat and stir in all the remaining ingredients except the parsley. Simmer for 1 minute. Serve hot or cold, sprinkled with parsley.

OKRA IN OIL

This is a traditional Lenten dish in Arab countries. It is usually served cold.

200g/8oz **WHOLE OKRA, WASHED AND TRIMMED**
125ml/5fl oz/⅔ cup **OLIVE OIL**
1 **ONION, FINELY CHOPPED**
3 cloves **GARLIC, FINELY CHOPPED**
2 teaspoons **WHOLE CORIANDER SEEDS**
SALT AND PEPPER
2 tablespoons **TOMATO PUREE**
125ml/5fl oz/⅔ cup **WATER**
JUICE OF 1 LEMON

Fry the *okra* in olive oil until lightly browned. Remove from the pan with a slotted spoon. Add the onion and garlic and fry until soft. Return the *okra* to the pan together with all the remaining ingredients, except the lemon juice. Bring to the boil and simmer for 10 minutes; do not overcook or the *okra* will break up. Finally, stir in the lemon juice and leave to cool before serving.

Variation

■ *Haricot* beans, turnips and leeks can all be effectively prepared in this way.

CHICKEN BREASTS WITH OLIVES AND FONTINA CHEESE

4 CHICKEN BREASTS
FLOUR, SEASONED
BUTTER
4 thin slices FONTINA CHEESE
4 tablespoons OLIVE PASTE

Toss the chicken breasts in seasoned flour and fry in butter until cooked through. When cooked, place a thin slice of cheese on each breast and top with olive paste. Turn off the heat and cover with a lid for a minute or so. Serve as soon as the cheese melts and begins to blend with the olive paste.

CHICKEN WITH ALMONDS

4 CHICKEN BREAST FILLETS
2 tablespoons ALMOND OIL
I RED PEPPER, SEEDED AND SHREDDED
3 tablespoons WHOLE ALMONDS
I teaspoon TARRAGON, FRESHLY CHOPPED
125ml/5fl oz/⅔ cup SINGLE OR LIGHT CREAM
SALT AND PEPPER

Slice the chicken breast fillets fairly thinly. Heat the oil in a pan and flash-fry the chicken with the pepper, almonds and tarragon. The chicken will take only about 5 minutes to cook. Pour on the cream and season. Bring to the boil and cook for 1 minute to thicken the sauce. Serve at once.

JAPANESE VINEGARED RICE

This *Sumeshi* rice is used for all Japanese *Sushi* cold rice dishes. These may be as simple as a small ball of rice wrapped in seaweed or topped with a little raw fish.

350g/12oz/2 cups JAPANESE SHORT-GRAIN RICE
50ml/2fl oz/¼ cup RICE VINEGAR
1½ tablespoons SUGAR
I teaspoon SALT

Wash the rice thoroughly and then drain in a fine sieve for about 1 hour. Transfer the rice to a saucepan and cover with 450ml/¾ pint water. Bring quickly to the boil. Cover and simmer gently for 15 minutes. Remove the pan from the heat, keeping tightly closed, and leave to stand for a further 10-15 minutes. Mix the vinegar with the sugar and salt, and stir until they are dissolved. Transfer the cooked rice to a bowl and carefully fold in the vinegar mixture. Leave to cool.

TROUT WITH HAZELNUTS

4 TROUT, CLEANED AND WASHED
SALT AND PEPPER
4 tablespoons **HAZELNUT OIL**
75g/3oz/¾ cup **HAZELNUTS, CHOPPED AND WASHED**
WHITE WINE (OPTIONAL)
I tablespoon **CHERVIL, FRESHLY CHOPPED**

Slash the trout twice on each side with a sharp knife and season. Heat the oil in a large frying pan and fry the trout for 5-8 minutes on each side, depending on size, until cooked. Remove the fish from the pan and keep warm. Add the hazelnuts to the pan and heat in the juices, adding a little water or white wine if more liquid is needed. Spoon over the fish and sprinkle with chervil. Serve at once.

Variations

■ Almond or walnut oil can be used in place of hazelnut oil, together with the appropriate nuts.

■ Sardines and sprats can also be cooked in this way.

MARINATED MONKFISH

This *Tapas* recipe from Spain makes a very good appetizer.

450g/1lb **MONKFISH, FILLETED**
2 cloves **GARLIC, PEELED AND FINELY CHOPPED**
100ml/4fl oz/½ cup **WHITE WINE VINEGAR**
100ml/4fl oz/½ cup **OLIVE OIL**
I **BAYLEAF, CRUSHED**
I teaspoon **HOT PAPRIKA**
I pinch **DRIED OREGANO**
SALT

Cut the monkfish into small even-sized pieces and place in a shallow dish. Mix all the remaining ingredients and pour over the top. Cover and leave to stand for 3-4 hours. Drain the fish cubes and fry in fresh olive oil, or skewer on cocktail sticks and then grill on each side for 1-2 minutes, depending on size. Serve hot.

LOIN OF PORK WITH MUSTARD

Any kind of mustard can be used for this recipe.

1½kg/3lb LOIN OF PORK JOINT, WITH THE SKIN AND MOST OF THE FAT REMOVED

2 tablespoons MUSTARD

2 tablespoons CLEAR HONEY

1 tablespoon WALNUT OR HAZELNUT OIL

Set the oven to 220°C/425°F/Gas Mark 7. Place the joint on a rack over a roasting tin. Mix all the remaining ingredients and brush all over the outside of the pork. Roast for 2 hours, covering with foil if the pork shows signs of burning. Place the pork on a serving plate. Drain the fat off and use the meat juices in the gravy.

INDEX

Entries for recipes are in italics.